CERTAIN SMALL WORKS

Certain Small Works

BY ROBERT H. TAYLOR

WITH AN INTRODUCTION BY
JEREMIAH S. FINCH

PRINCETON, NEW JERSEY
PRINCETON UNIVERSITY LIBRARY
1980

Copyright © 1980 by Princeton University Library
ISBN no. 0-87811-023-2
Library of Congress catalogue card no. 79-3891

Designed by Bruce D. Campbell
Printed in the United States of America
by Princeton University Press at Princeton, New Jersey

Contents

Acknowledgment	vi
Author's Note	vii
Introduction BY JEREMIAH S. FINCH	ix
I. OF COLLECTORS AND COLLECTING	1
How It Began	3
Il Convivio	11
The J. Harlin O'Connell Collection	21
Bibliothecohimatiourgomachia	27
The Common Habitation	36
II. THE WRITER'S CRAFT	49
Authors at Work	51
The Singular Anomalies	69
Max Beerbohm's Literary Credo	83
III. ANTHONY TROLLOPE	99
On Rereading *Barchester Towers*	101
The Morris L. Parrish Trollope Collection	108
The Trollopes Write to Bentley	116
Trollope as Dramatist	157

ACKNOWLEDGMENT

For permission to reprint these essays and their illustrations, I am greatly indebted to the following: the Grolier Club, the Bibliographical Society of America, the Book Collector, the Princeton University Library Chronicle, the Trollopian, the Oxford University Press, and to Mr. Rupert Hart-Davis and Mr. Herman W. Liebert.

AUTHOR'S NOTE

I have stolen the title of this volume. Following the theory that everything which needs to be said has been said already, I took it from a book of verse by Samuel Daniel printed in 1611, and reproduce the title here.

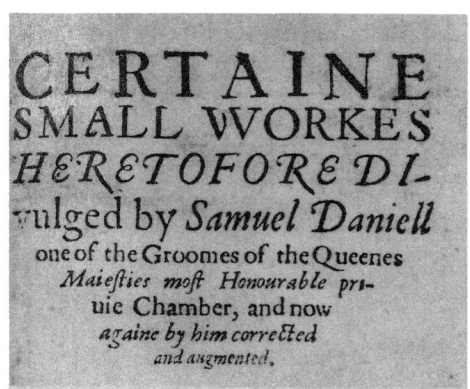

It seems to me very apposite. I have divulged these pieces at a number of different places over a great many years, and this gathering of them is not wholly an act of vanity but something of a memorial to the pleasure I had in writing them. I hope that the reader may even now find some enjoyment in leafing through these pages.

Robert H. Taylor

Introduction

In these pleasant essays and addresses Robert Taylor tells of his adventures in the world of books with wit, grace, and a ready smile. He is one of those rare collectors who actually reads his books and writes about them with distinction. His integrity as a collector is not "sullied by authorship," as one bookman timidly put it on venturing into print; careful scholarship is reflected in many a wise comment. Friends and acquaintances will find his printed words as lively as his conversation. Every page attests to a keen mind and a good nature.

One does not read far without discovering that the author has a special gift of phrase. He speaks of the Brontë sisters' "strange, smoldering personalities." In "How it Began" he tells how he tried to gather contemporary editions and "in the process stretched the word well out of joint." Having laboriously collated the manuscript of a Trollope novel with the printed text for an article to be published by the *Bibliographical Society of America*, he was then told to "make it funny." This reduced him to "a cataleptic condition from which I am still suffering."

As these examples suggest, his sense of humor is ever ready. He narrates that when visiting Grolier Club members were informed that the Italian government recognized the group as representatives of American culture, "a stupefied silence" followed. He can laugh at himself: "the collector is sentimental, illogical, selfish, extravagant, capricious." When scolded by a dealer, "You're just like every other God-damned collector," he reflects that he "does not ask for any better tribute."

Do not think, however, that his is effortless writing. One brief sentence can introduce a subject and set forth a theme. "Anyone discussing him [Max Beerbohm] must cling to a few such indisputable facts because he is surrounded by so many inexplicable paradoxes." Moreover, there is the literary historian in Robert Taylor: "Indeed, the decade of 1890-1900 appears at times like the Romantic Period seen through the wrong end of a jewelled opera glass." Speaking of Trollope, he observes that "the trivia of earlier times . . . make up the changing surface of all civilizations." His command of a wide range of authors is displayed when he gathers Tennyson, Swinburne, Kipling, James, Galsworthy, Meredith, and others into one breathless but ample paragraph.

Although he disclaims any standing as a scholar, he consistently reveals scholarly instincts and scholarly habits. Never quite concealed by his lighthearted manner is a passion for exactness in matters bibliographical and a conviction that devoting one's life to books is a serious matter; in Browning's Fra Lippo Lippi's words, "it means intensely and means good." He knows his writers intimately. In "Authors at Work" Pope is his near neighbor, Tennyson not far off, Sheridan just around the corner, and Emily Dickinson the girl next door. Plato, Housman, Burns, and Stevenson rub elbows quite comfortably. When he turns to lady novelists, he shows a sympathetic awareness of the problems they faced, and he seems to hear "the faint, constant scratching of many pens."

Mild mannered he is, but he can let fly a resounding curse—or at least a hope—that autograph hounds who cut up manuscript letters are "all frizzling in hell." Not all authors please him. He joins the ranks of the blessed (in this writer's opinion) when he confesses that Carlyle is "not exactly a favorite." His animadversions are usually gentler, though always discerning and just. Most readers of *Barchester Towers* will agree with his remark about Eleanor Bold's "too easy tears." On a larger scale, he can offer good critical comments that invite ready acceptance, as when he observes that Trollope's methods as a novelist "too frequently . . . resulted in a rather shapeless structure."

Robert Taylor is the last person to be sententious, yet there is a quiet confidence and sagacity in many a passing remark.

He reflects that "books represent part of our inheritance of wisdom and beauty." He wonders that "the nature of genius remains incomprehensible." One hears a faint echo of Sir Thomas Browne in the wistful observation that "Everything, including books and ideas, is in a furious race with oblivion." He is not afraid to admit a note of sadness when he says of *fin-de-siècle* writers: "if some of their gold leaf has peeled away, and if some of the purple cloth has faded . . . it is no great matter." Unobstrusively, he coins an epigram: "education is sometimes obtained in spite of one's self."

The esteem in which he is held is reflected in the issue of *The Princeton University Library Chronicle* entirely devoted to him and to his collection. In these essays he is variously referred to as "Mr. Taylor," "Robert Taylor," and "Bob"— but always with respect and with affection. As an old friend, Mary Hyde, wrote in that volume, he is "a great bookman, and one who is loved by other collectors."

When Coleridge once asked Charles Lamb, "Have you ever heard me preach, Charles?" Lamb stammered, "I n- never heard you do anything else!" Robert Taylor does not preach. He simply communicates, by his gift of expression, his pleasure in his books and everything to do with them. It is all accomplished with pervasive modesty, aptly suggested in his title, "Certain Small Works." The reader will find these "Small Works" large in enjoyment.

Jeremiah S. Finch

I

OF COLLECTORS AND COLLECTING

How It Began

During my last year in prep school an astonishing new student joined our class. Though contemptuous of sports, he was respected by the athletes; though brilliant scholastically, he took his work lightly; above all, he was the most dazzlingly sophisticated creature imaginable. With awe I watched as he ignored any rule that interfered with his personal convenience, or read the *Decameron* aloud in the dormitory for shock value, or uttered dogmatic defences of contemporary painting and *Ulysses*. This was in 1925-6, the era of Mencken and Gertrude Stein and the founding of the *New Yorker*; and I rejoiced in the knowledge that under his guidance I too had become an emancipated soul, a man of the world at last.

But there was another discovery I made with his help: old books. At the shop of Edgar H. Wells, where my friend was known, I bought my first rarity. It was a 1794 edition of Johnson's *Lives*, four volumes in eighteenth-century calf, whose pages were slightly yellow, but whose generous type remained clear and legible. It was the first tangible link with the past which I had ever possessed, and I pored over it most of the night, reminding myself frequently that this was the way the work had looked to its original readers. In the morning I displayed it to my friend and promptly encountered another aspect of collecting. Having cracked Wells's code, he glanced at the front end-paper and with a superior smile told me what Wells had paid for it. I am probably the only collector who, within twenty-four hours of buying his first rare book, learned the dealer's profit.

However, with A. E. Newton's *Amenities* as a spur, even this did not deter me long. I bought a few modern first editions, such as *Antic Hay* and *Those Barren Leaves*, since they

This description appeared in the Winter 1954 issue of The Book Collector.

cost comparatively little, but I was happier with older books. I deliberated over the first collected Congreve. The term puzzled me: did it mean, perhaps, the earliest edition that collectors bothered with? I would have to find out—but certainly not by asking, which would betray ignorance. My allowance would cover only an occasional item, and I felt that prices (soon to reach their zenith in the Kern Sale) would forever keep the books I really wanted out of my financial reach. Therefore I tried to gather 'contemporary' editions of them—and in the process stretched the word well out of joint. All I required was that an eighteenth-century book be in an eighteenth-century edition, and the Stockdale *Robinson Crusoe* of 1790 was as good, for my purpose, as the first edition of 1719.

Desultory acquisitions of this nature continued to give me pleasure, although there were periods when other interests prevailed. It was early in my second year at Princeton that I discovered the enjoyment offered by Trollope's novels, as well as the fact that no complete set of his works existed. If I hoped to own even reading copies I would have to try for first editions, since many of his books existed in no other form. The difficulty was the cost. 'But,' I thought, 'if I am careful to buy badly worn copies I may one day be able to have them bound as a respectable set.' With this in mind I set out to assemble cripples, and promptly learned the convenience of having a name with which to answer the bookseller's inevitable query: 'Is there anything in particular I can show you?' There was much else to learn, but I was too ignorant even to be aware of that. I recall refusing to buy Michael Sadleir's bibliography of Trollope. It seemed largely composed of incomprehensible gibberish, and for the price (ten dollars) I could certainly obtain one, perhaps two, items I really wanted. The depression was making itself felt, and any act of purchase carried with it a sense of extravagance. Not until some time afterwards did I find out the value of such a bibliography.

However, education is sometimes obtained in spite of oneself. I ventured occasionally into the auction rooms, and one day bought a bundle of three Trollope novels, and, on getting them home, realized that one was too good to rebind. Had I had any notion of the expense into which that book would ultimately plunge me, I would have destroyed it instantly. But it stayed with the others, making them look shabby and undesirable. Of course I knew condition to be a factor in the price of old books, but never before had the reason for it been made so clear to me. Couldn't I perhaps get better copies and forego the rebinding project? After all, rebinding might also prove to be expensive.

And then I stumbled on two or three shelves of Trollope which a dealer was selling on consignment. That completed my conversion. Moreover, the dealer extracted from me the admission that I was interested in other things. Thereafter, only a depleted bank balance could stop my miscellaneous buying. *The Way of the World* would be followed by *The Way of All Flesh*, a presentation *Paracelsus* by *Two Years before the Mast*, an inferior Second Folio by *Leaves of Grass*. Since enthusiasts always encounter opportunity, I went quite by chance to the opening of the Hearst sale at Gimbel's department store in January 1941. Every kind of *objet d'art* in the world appeared to be offered to the public, confusing the regular customers and sales-girls alike. There was not a great deal to beguile the book-collector, but two Trollope manuscripts were for sale. I could afford only the cheaper, alas, but over that one, *The American Senator*, I did not hesitate. I now have nine, but that was probably the only bargain in the lot. I also purchased there a letter of Charlotte Brontë, the nine-page miniature autobiography which she wrote on 31 July 1848, to W. S. Williams. Although I have since been offered a good many of her letters, these have all been less interesting and more expensive.

By this time I had met other collectors, notably Carroll Wilson, whose enthusiasm and encouragement were exactly of that knowledgeable sort which every beginner should encounter and too seldom does. And apart from the routine instruction which his books gave me, they provided a source of comfort. I had learned that every good collector should have a plan: he ought to collect in scholarly fashion everything by or about one man or one period; he ought to collect work of the 'Nineties, or Restoration Drama, or the history of astronomy, or Victorian book-illustrations. Carroll collected chiefly New England authors; but in addition he had a passion for the first appearance of familiar quotations—a highly personal selection—which produced a heterogeneous group on his shelves, and he also had a number of books he simply liked. These items were a great solace to me; and as I added *Hans Brinker* to Percy's *Reliques*, and *The Mill on the Floss* to *The Beaux' Stratagem*, I ceased to worry about the chaos in my own bookcases.

A superb five-circle *Autocrat* turned up; so did variant bindings of Beerbohm's *More*; so did *She Stoops to Conquer*; so did *Huckleberry Finn* in sheep (a convenient way out of the green-versus-blue cloth controversy). None of these seemed to bear any relation to one another, yet all of them were books I wanted. Finally I realized that I was collecting English and American literature. Though this implied an infinitely vaster library than I could ever hope to assemble, no more limited description would be accurate.

It was an erratic collection, and would never be large, but I resolved that every important author or period would be represented by at least one item which could also form the basis of a larger group if ever it were possible to expand. Carlyle, for example, is not exactly a favourite of mine, but he was an undeniably important figure of the nineteenth century. I have, therefore, a presentation copy of the 1834 *Sartor Resartus*, which would be a key book in any Carlyle collection, but which by itself can represent its author.

Certain seventeenth-century titles had begun to come my way: *Lucasta*, Coryat's *Crudities*, Sir Thomas Browne's *Pseudodoxia Epidemica*, and Carew's *Poems*, all first editions in contemporary calf; but when I started to add a few sixteenth-century books, such as the 1532 *Confessio Amantis* and *The Faerie Queene*, I became a little frightened. Where was all this leading?

# SARTOR RESARTUS.

IN THREE BOOKS.

Reprinted for Friends from Fraser's Magazine.

Mein Vermächtniss, wie herrlich weit und breit!
Die Zeit ist mein Vermächtniss, mein Acker ist die Zeit.

LONDON:
JAMES FRASER, 215 REGENT STREET.

M.DCCC.XXXIV.

Presentation Copy of *Sartor Resartus* (1834).

It led to a new library, a room added to my home. Building costs effectively curtailed purchases for a while, but eventually they recommenced: the 1859 *Rubaiyat*, the 1589 Hakluyt, *Sense and Sensibility* in boards, Gray's *Elegy* bound with other eighteenth-century items, *Songs of Innocence*, the 1532 Chaucer, the 1559 *Mirror for Magistrates*, all found their way in. So did a presentation *Vanity Fair*, Skelton's *Why Come Ye Nat to Court?* (?1560), a 1620 *Faustus*, *Wuthering Heights* (without *Agnes Grey*), *The Knight of the Burning Pestle*, Gray's *Ode on a Distant Prospect*, the Bristol *Lyrical Ballads*, and *Pamela*.

Whenever it was possible I now tried to get seventeenth-century or later books in original or contemporary binding. My copies of Donne's *Devotions* and the 1633 *Poems*, *The Anatomy of Melancholy*, Chapman's *Homer* (?1609) and Cornwallis's *Essays* are all in contemporary vellum. *Lycidas* and *Areopagitica* are in modern levant, the chance of finding them otherwise being negligible; but I have managed to secure in contemporary calf *Paradise Lost* (the first and second title-pages), the 1645 *Poems*, the 1673 *Poems* (both imprints), and *Paradise Regained*. Keats's three volumes[1] and Hazlitt's *Round Table* (the Bellew copy) are all in boards. And each Virginia Woolf item has its proper dust-jacket, with the exception of *The Voyage Out*, which appears to be in a trial binding. There are unhappy deviations from this ideal, of course; but I maintain it is better to have a rebound *Adventures of a Younger Son* than no copy at all—and that, practically, is the choice most of us are faced with. There is not quite the same excuse for a rebound *Confessions of a Thug*—but then, allowances must be made for a dedication copy. And if my Pisa *Adonais* is not in wrappers, it is at least uncut, with the lines 'Swifter far than summer's flight' in Shelley's hand on one of the back flyleaves.

[1] Since writing this, the copy of *Poems* has been replaced by the copy (formerly in the Hogan Collection) inscribed by Keats to Wordsworth, covered (probably by Mrs. Wordsworth), in 'Lakeland Petticoat' in the 'Cottonian' style.

Recently I have begun to assemble significant landmarks in English biography, with a presentation *Life of Johnson* as a cornerstone. It is pleasant to find that fascinating books, like Cibber's *Apology* and Gosse's *Father and Son* are still inexpensive and easily met with. Cavendish's *Wolsey*, Mrs. Gaskell's *Charlotte Brontë*, and Forster's *Dickens* may require a little more searching, but Lockhart's *Scott* is to be had almost anywhere. This field has never been so thoroughly gleaned as most others, and is consequently very rewarding—up to the period of the dull, official two-volume Life-and-Letters.

The word 'letters' reminds me that my gathering of autograph material was given impetus by the purchase of the John Wild collection. Of some 2400 items I retained only the seventy-five or so which had literary interest; but among these is a letter from Sterne to Dodsley offering him *Tristram Shandy*, one from Goldsmith to John Nourse, one from Burns to William Nichol—and there are others, less important, from Marvell, Fielding, Pope, Gay, Thomson, Sheridan, Hume, Walpole, Richardson, Byron, Crabbe, Coleridge, Shelley, and a host of minor people.

Other letters were added subsequently: single specimens from Sir Thomas Browne, Waller, Defoe, Jane Austen, Keats, George Eliot and Henry James; several from Pepys, Scott, Dickens, Tennyson, Thackeray, Wilde, Beerbohm, Shaw, and about one hundred and twenty-five from Trollope together with a number from his mother and other relatives. Except in a few cases, I have tried to limit myself to letters which refer to the author's work or else have some biographical value.

Manuscripts include a short story by Wilkie Collins; the brief beginnings of two unfinished novels by Charlotte Brontë as well as one example of each of her juvenile prose and verse, and poems by her sister Anne; two instalments of *The Uncommercial Traveller*; the material Gray sent to the Foulis Press for that edition of his poems; O'Shaughnessy's *We Are the Music-Makers*; the manuscript and pencil draft of *Zuleika Dobson*; three Swinburne lyrics; a couple of Beerbohm essays, one essay by Lytton Strachey and one by Shaw; and, more recent and splendid, the first draft of *The School for Scandal*.

I have by now so splattered the big names about that a magnificently erroneous impression has been given. This is, once again, a collection of books that I like, and not only are a great many unimportant volumes elbowing their more illustrious brethren on the shelves, but some standard items which I don't care for—e.g., *Of Human Bondage* and Chesterfield's *Letters*—will never be there. In reality, the butter is spread very thin, and a list of serious gaps would be far longer than this account indicates. A great many years of collecting have not sufficed to track down all the Trollope titles that I want (although *The Macdermots of Ballycloran* was added in 1947), and I am still engaged in the heart-breaking business of replacing inferior copies of his novels with better ones as they come along. Besides, if I may repeat a lament that echoes down the centuries, it is impossible to procure certain books nowadays. *Comus*, to mention only one, is unobtainable, and what is to be done about Shakespeare? The 1640 *Poems* and two Pavier forgeries are excellent things to have, certainly, but they are no more than cousins, at least once removed, of the great and wonderful volumes so few collectors have ever been privileged to own. The key book, of course, is obvious, but I am resigned to the fact that a First Folio will always be too dear for my possessing.

Incidentally, I do know where there is a Shakespeare quarto to be had, if one had but the money to buy it. True, a single quarto will not make a collection, but that is the beauty of my system: it would *represent* Shakespeare, represent him very well indeed . . . A pity that the price . . . Perhaps, after all, I should consider . . . But no. No, let us be sensible.

Il Convivio

The first social event of our trip was the foregathering at the Grolier Club before our departure for Idlewild. We milled about on the familiar sidewalk with that blend of gregarious excitement and self-conscious restraint which infects all group travelers at their initial encounter. Lovett supplied copious tap-water for the thirsty—a beverage we were largely to ignore in the days ahead. Yet our first attempt to do just this, an hour or so later in the Swissair lounge, met defeat. The single harried bartender there was apparently expecting a Methodist synod, and his efforts to cope with the urgent needs of the Grolier *amici* were pathetically inadequate. Those who secured limp potato chips and a modicum of whiskey (rumored to be Old Confusion) were at that moment considered lucky. Never again, during three fabulous and fascinating weeks, were we to be so ill-lodged, ill-fed or ill-refreshed.

With the unfurling of what may have been the world's first calligraphic banner *EX LIBRIS 2* (the work of a gifted fellow member) we emplaned. A brief period of turning about in the seats like settling dogs, and we were airborne; cocktails and dinner followed shortly. The component parts of the latter had been christened with appropriate names in advance by a member, and Swissair authorities had accepted them: Salza 'alla Trivulziana,' Filetto di Bue 'Poldi Pezzoli,' and so on—but they thought it safer not to include his Gritti toast.

Immediately afterwards President Hyde delivered over the loudspeaker his official messages. This was not merely a pleasure trip, he told us; we had the blessing of the State

Written in collaboration with Herman W. Liebert (now librarian emeritus of the Beinecke Library of Yale University), this account of the hospitality enjoyed by Grolier Club members during their trip to Italy in 1962 appeared originally in the Club's publication Iter Italicum *(New York, 1963).*

Department and we were officially recognized by the Italian government as representatives of American culture. In the stupefied silence that followed he reminded us that it would be well to avoid political discussion. This, most of us felt, would be easy, especially in Italian; and in the brief time that separated dinner from dawn we comfortably forgot about being intellectual ambassadors.

But the very next day required us to behave as though we were. Dr. Piantanida, of the Circolo dei Librai Antiquari, had arranged a reception at the Poldi Pezzoli Museum in Milan, and there we were told in an impressive speech that Milan had the honor of welcoming the first cultural group from the United States ever to visit Italy. We were greatly moved, and also overcome by a sense of our unworthiness.

On the terrace facing the beautiful courtyard, we experienced our first vista of the endless and festive tables of the Italian buffet, piled high with goblets whose multicolored contents we learned to identify as Campari, Americano, Negroni, succo di frutta, and a disguised old friend, *dgeen*. They flanked a bewildering variety of canapés as delectable as they were mysterious—though we had no trouble in identifying the half-dollar sized pizzas. Here too began the cry for that commodity so necessary to our refrigerated American palates: *più di ghiaccio, per favore!*

This was also our first experience with what was soon known as The Presentation: our endeavor to thank our hosts, however inadequately, with gifts of Grolier Club publications (*Grolier 75* and *Italian Influence on American Literature*) to the accompaniment of speeches. This heartfelt oratory was sometimes delivered in English, sometimes in Italian, the latter ranging from the purest *lingua toscana* to what may possibly have been Etruscan.

Next day another reception was tendered us at the handsome Villa Reale (where Petrarch's Laura is buried, say the Milanese). From the windows in the rear could be seen a charming *tempietto d'amore* amid the ever-present grass and trees that, though hidden from the streets, so lavishly adorn

Italian cities. Our announced host, the Sindaco, had disappeared, perhaps through an opening to the right or left, but his deputy received us with full municipal honors. For the first of many times our secretary produced the Italian speech he had smuggled through customs; his pause for the translator, after the first mushroom cloud of rhetoric, was greeted by the silence of absolute incomprehension, and his protestation that all the words were in the back of his first-year Italian grammar was lost in a burst of amiable laughter. We dutifully avoided political discussion, concentrating instead so hard on the refreshments as to suggest that we had never before seen any.

A cocktail party the following afternoon given for us by Carlo Alberto Chiesa, our Virgil, foreshadowed the unceasing attention he would pay to our needs for the rest of the trip. Here, in his lovely studio on the Via Bigli, he was presented with an owl in Steuben glass as a small token of our gratitude, and here we enjoyed drinks and canapés while looking over his terrace to the garden beyond.

We were what our schedule ironically called 'at leisure' that evening for dinner (the opera began late), and this allowed us to sample at various restaurants such regional specialties as ossobuco, the superb gorgonzola and a variety of Italian wines—Valpolicella, Bardolino, Soave—which led us to lament how ill these nectars traveled.

The next day we regretfully left Milan for Verona, and went to an attractive inn, high on a hill above the city, to prepare for the grand luncheons to follow. Aperitifs were served during a time insufficient even to admire the view properly. Then we were dragged away and divided in two groups, each going to a great Veronese house that had offered us hospitality. Of our kind hosts, the Galtarossas and the Fagiuolis, what praise can be enough? Where else may one dine today on food and drink all produced on the proprietor's own land? In addition, Dr. Fagiuoli had had printed for us a memento, a reproduction of the title page of Luca Pacioli's *Summa de Arithmetica* (Toscolano, 1523), in which the printer refers to this region as the only place in the world where one may get carpione, the fish we were served. This was accompanied by a leaflet in Latin and English, the work of the younger Fagiuolis, telling the story of this delicacy. The carpione, however, was but one of many mouthwatering dishes. Humbler foods, such as salame and polenta (prepared by our hostess) could, we learned, be transmuted into something very different from their usual incarnation, and everything was as pleasing to the eye as it was to the taste buds. We marveled as we realized that each of these generous families had given such a feast to some seventy complete strangers. Long were the fruitless arguments afterwards as to which meal was the more magnificent, and perhaps it is enough to say that no guest would have foregone his own experience no matter how glowingly the other affair was described to him.

Venice confirmed the belief of many members that water was made to run under bridges. The evening of our arrival allowed some of us to learn the delights of a strega or a brandy in the Piazza San Marco, the finest drawing room of Europe, and many were the greetings between Grolierites as the crowd flowed round the square.

The luxury of our own boat to the island of Torcello the next day was but the preface of luxe to come. At the Locanda Cipriani—*ambiente caratteristico in un angolo fiorito*—Dr. Dario Roma, of the Tourist Office, gave us a lunch fit for the ancient local saints. On more than one tongue the cannelloni yet linger as an enchanted memory. A thoughtful member voiced what might well have become the motto of the trip: 'I have no business eating this.' His sentiment, however true, did not deter him nor any of us, then or later, from the almost continuous ingestion of delicacies. Those who were still ambulatory walked the few hundred yards back to our launch; the rest were grateful for transportation by gondola.

In Venice, too, we were at our first approach to the littoral, and learned what was to delight us for the rest of the trip: pesce and frutti di mare. Perhaps only a bibliophile can fully appreciate sea foods delicately cooked to just the color of contemporary calf.

In Ferrara, at the Hotel Astra, we made an effort to be hosts ourselves, and our chief guest, General Ugo Malagù, honored us with a speech in English that made nearly all of us blush for our halting command of his tongue.

At Rimini that night, the arrival of a hundred-odd thirsty Grolierites at a three-stool bar attended by a part-time bartender left some throats temporarily unassuaged, but it did not take long for insistent demands to undam the flow. Some of our more traveled members took advantage of their local knowledge, and at the Vecchia Rimini restaurant reveled in sogliola alla matriciana, calamari alla tarantina and the fine white Verdicchio.

The next day at Cesena we were again hosts at the celebrated Ristorante Casali, where gastronomy, unlike the books at the library, was wholly unchained. The menus printed on silk named the seven delicious courses and the three wines, but made no mention of the live goldfish that swam at the base of each lady's dessert-glass!

From Cesena some of us went over the hills to Florence, while the less adventurous took the low road via Bologna, where the book fair obligingly staged in the Piazza was one of the unscheduled social events, and some of us learned the significance of *albergo diurno*.

At Florence, our fellow member Silvain Brunschwig and his wife gave us a reception in their villa at Bagno a Ripoli. They were disappointed in the weather, fearing that we would find it too chilly to stay in the garden, so carefully prepared for us; but a sizable number of us found it, like the villa's interior, both comfortable and lovely. The hospitality, the books and the panoramic view of the city remain vividly in our memory.

In such Florentine moments as we had at leisure, we sampled specialties like bistecca alla fiorentina, and were able to enjoy Chianti at home, where it is never better.

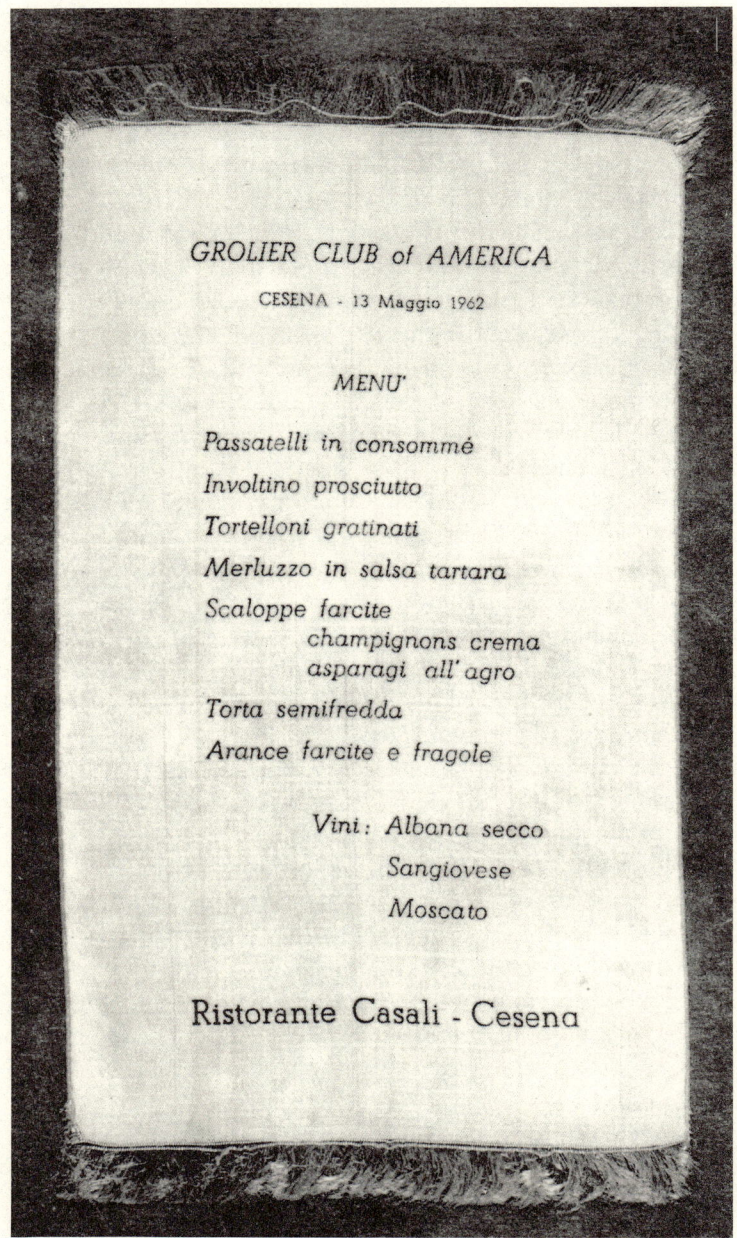

Menu of the luncheon consumed by the Grolier Club at Cesena.

The delicious luncheon tendered us at Forte Belvedere by Commendatore Vannini-Parenti, to which we were escorted by a splendid guard of honor in fifteenth-century dress with halberds and banners amid a roll of drums, gave us some sense of what we had missed by being born in the wrong age. There were a few moments afterwards for a short stroll on the ramparts to admire still a different view of Florence before we were drummed to the buses.

Our climactic experience in Florence was the reception given us by our guardian angel, Commendatore de Marinis, at his house, the Villa Montalto. Four hundred Florentines were invited to meet us, and so enormous was that palatial mansion that the rooms seemed only pleasantly occupied. On this occasion the four officers of the Club paid tribute to the man who had planned our trip and shepherded us through our daze of entertainment with an energy the despair of his juniors. He was presented with a Steuben glass star which contained the Club's crest as well as the two Club publications. The tape recorder which was to perpetuate this ceremony did not function, and on the whole this was a good thing: what could it display except our own inadequate expressions of gratitude? Meanwhile, the treasures of the de Marinis collection were ours to wonder at, his gardens were ours to wander in and once more we tried vainly to imagine how such hospitality could ever be repaid.

Like Forte Belvedere, the Palazzo Vecchio, its courtyard aflame with azaleas, took us back to a more regal day. Here, as guests of the Mayor, Professore La Pira, we received with delight his fluent rhetoric, of which his expressive pantomime gave us a very fair translation. Subsequent refreshments—three flights up—among the quattrocento glories of the Hall of Lilies were equally satisfying.

Again the *EX LIBRIS* 2 banner was unfurled, this time in the railroad station, as we reluctantly moved forward on our travels. Even when under way our enjoyment of good food, good wine and good fellowship was not interrupted: lunch on our special train from Florence to Naples left us regretting that they did not order these matters better at home.

Here we were just past the halfway mark, and those making their visit had already learned some Italian ways. Those wishing salt or pepper knew now that they must be asked for; that San Pelligrino had bubbles and Fiuggi did not; and that martinis were served in the special product of a medieval thimble factory. But how much more we had learned that was good: that no form of pasta needed to taste like wet shelf-paper, as at home; that dinner was very agreeable with two wines, and better with three; and that it was foolish to choose *between* cheese and fruit when both were so delicious.

Our gustatory landmark at Naples was the luncheon given us by the civic authorities, with Signor Mario Mastrolilli presiding as host, at the renowned restaurant Le Arcate, where the *vista estera eccezionalmente amena* of the city and the sea matched even the cuisine. We rejoiced in arragosta, lupo di mare and a succession of wines.

The next day we reached our southernmost point, and if the fascination of Pompeii and Herculaneum left us a little dry, the luncheon at the Hotel La Baia at Vietri sul Mare, near Salerno, did not. We understood why St. Matthew had resided there since 954, and the more greedy of us were glad to recall that Salerno was the fons medicinae of the Hippocratic school.

And then to Rome. We had barely time after our arrival to get our *abiti scuri* pressed before we were due at the Villa Madama. This edifice, built from designs by Raphael, is used now only for government entertaining, and is not open to the public. The public, we felt, misses a great deal: it is a beautiful palazzo with gardens once famous and now restored to their former grandeur, and in this setting was provided the most magnificent of all our receptions. We were greeted by the Onorevole Carlo Russo, Undersecretary for Foreign Affairs (the Secretary having very recently become President), and by our fellow member, Cardinal Tisserant, who in his scarlet robes was a dazzling figure. Indeed, talking with him was like conversing with a Titian portrait. And when the company—

this included many Roman guests—had progressed through various spacious rooms, the doors of the banquet hall were thrown open to disclose, in that splendid apartment, a table sixty feet long covered with every conceivable edible. A similar range of drinks was offered, and those who were clever enough to discover the Marsala dated 1840 were wise enough to keep it to themselves. Aurum potabile! After dining there was time for a leisurely walk through some of the moonlit gardens, past statues and cypresses, fountains and clipped box. Never did we leave any place more unwillingly.

Our American hosts in Rome were no less kind. After our visit to the American Academy, Mr. and Mrs. Richard Kimball entertained us at the Villa Aurelia. We were made free of the whole top floor, including the ballroom, and, relaxing in the familiar atmosphere of a cocktail party, we admired from the windows the beautiful views of Rome. Two days later Ambassador and Mrs. Reinhardt gave a reception for us at the Villa Taverna. Again we were treated with infinite hospitality, and wandered, glass in hand, through enchanting gardens in the twilight.

And just as we thought that nothing could be more spectacular than what we had experienced in the last three weeks, our fellow member Halsted VanderPoel proved that there was by arranging a dinner for us at the Castel Sant'Angelo. (Not even our Italian friends could believe it: this privilege was never granted before to a private person.) Flambeaux lit the stairs as we climbed to the ramparts on which were posted guards in sixteenth-century costume. After cocktails in Julius II's loggia, designed by Bramante, we were seated at tables in the Biblioteca and Cagliostra, where we drank and dined with all the grandeur of the former inhabitants. After a few engaging speeches from our host and our president, we went out to the loggia of Paul III, discovering still more refreshments there. The views were as heady as the drinks, for under the moon and stars Rome was spread out below us, an incomparable picture. We could only marvel, wondering whether this or any episode of our fantastic journey had really taken place.

Our last day in Rome had originally been scheduled as 'free'; but, like nature, Commendatore de Marinis abhors a vacuum, and he quickly and firmly vetoed any notion of idleness. The morning found us walking through the ornate halls and magnificent rooms of the Palazzo Rospigliosi by invitation of the Princess Pallavicini. In the afternoon, the Prince and Princess Aldobrandini asked us to their villa at Frascati. The fountains, the flowers, the view looking over the quiet valleys of the Campagna, the kindness of our host, were all calculated to restore some of the nervous energy lost in the past hectic weeks.

The tour—the wildly, incredibly successful tour—was over. It really did happen, all of it: the sights, the buildings, the books, the manuscripts and, above all, the courtesy and hospitality of the country of *Il Cortegiano*. And as we recall its glories to warm our hearts again, perhaps we may like to sing with Bacchus, whom Francesco Redi brought back to Tuscany in 1685:

> Su su dunque in questo sangue
> Rinoviam l'arterie, e i musculi;
> E per chi s'invecchia, e langue
> Prepariam vetri maiusculi;
> Ed in festa baldanzosa
> Tra gli scherzi, e tra le risa
> Lasciam pur, lasciam passare
> Lui, che in numeri, e in misura
> Si ravvolge, e si consuma,
> E quaggiù Tempo si chiama;
> E bevendo, e ribevendo
> I pensier mandiamo in bando.
> *Bacco in Toscana*, 1685
> (Laurenziana, MS. Redi 193)

The J. Harlin O'Connell Collection

The nineteenth century opened with a magnificent outpouring of English lyric poetry; it closed, diminuendo, with curious minor echoes and inversions of its beginning. Indeed, the decade of 1890-1900 appears at times like the Romantic Period seen through the wrong end of a jeweled opera glass. Its most characteristic writers flourished for a briefer time, their talents were smaller, they lacked the energy and amplitude of their predecessors; but nevertheless many parallels remain, and even certain physical accidents are strikingly similar. One thinks of Beardsley dying, like Keats, of tuberculosis in his twenties; of Francis Thompson, like Coleridge, destroying his health with laudanum and talking interminably; of Davidson's body, like Shelley's, washed ashore; of Wilde attitudinizing like Byron and, like him, finding a Continental residence desirable for his last years because of scandal at home.

As in all periods of literary exuberance, youth was in revolt against the immediate past. The Romantics scorned the Augustan ideals, and the nineties decried Mid-Victorian virtues. And yet all such eras are necessarily influenced by their heritage: as the Gothic revival permeated the early years of the century, so did the Aesthetic movement color its end. Those writers who were *tout ce qu'il y a de plus fin-de-siècle* simply reversed the favorite theme of their great forerunners; they hymned the town rather than the country. Not for them the daffodils, the nightingale, the west wind: they celebrated Fleet Street, cosmetics, and "the iron lilies of the Strand." Nora of the Pavements dwelt among ways that were very thoroughly trodden, but she was as much a symbol as Lucy had been three

This article appeared first in The Princeton University Library Chronicle, *the spring-summer issue, 1958.*

generations earlier. Art and artifice were praised as never before. The label "decadent" was a banner to be carried proudly, with a self-consciousness that showed how vehemently the bearer wished to *épater les bourgeois*. There was an indefinable scent of patchouli in the air, an aroma of hothouse and boudoir. Wordsworth's primrose had become a green carnation.

The collection formed by the late J. Harlin O'Connell of the Princeton class of 1914, acquired by the Library in 1952 through the generosity of his daughter, Mrs. Pierre Matisse, illustrates with much charm this aspect of the nineties. Mr. O'Connell wrote an engaging account of it for the *Chronicle*,[1] and it is not the purpose of this article to repeat his remarks. But his modesty prevented him from indicating the scope of the collection, and a few statistics may therefore be allowable. There are in it more than twenty letters from Oscar Wilde, for example, most of them written in his late years, though one is as early as 1877; there are fourteen letters from Beardsley and eight of his drawings; seven letters from Beerbohm, together with three original caricatures and the manuscript of "On Speaking French"; eighteen letters from Ernest Dowson, plus the manuscripts of three of his poems; seventeen letters from Richard Le Gallienne; thirteen from Stephen Phillips, and the manuscript of *The King*; thirty-three from Frederick Wedmore; eleven from George Moore; and so on.

But such enumeration unfortunately cannot indicate their quality; nor does space allow a description of several single items which are particularly interesting. One, however, may perhaps represent its fellows. In my possession is a letter from Beerbohm to Gosse saying that because his parody of Henry James (in *A Christmas Garland*) contained "little or nothing of the great dark glow of the later manner," he was therefore enclosing four little pages of manuscript. "At the back of the upper edge of each page you will see an unpleasant streak of

[1] J. Harlin O'Connell '14, "A Collector Looks at the Nineties," *The Princeton University Library Chronicle*, II, No. 4 (June, 1941), 121-[132].

THE MOTE

struck Keith as lying near to, at indeed a hardly measurable distance from, the border-line of his patience. If she didn't _want_ the doll, why the deuce had she made such a point of getting it? He was perhaps on the verge of putting this question to her, when, waving her hand to include both stockings, she asked him, "Isn't what you mean — and what by the same token, my dear, _I_ mean it really s'ag_it_ of — rather, for us, situated 'plop' in the foreground?"

= He took the measure of this; he had fairly unreeled for it, like a little "surveyor" called in from round the corner, the long slick lineated tape; his interest in the verdict of which was now sufficiently attested by his silence. He was to break it, however, this silence, in the happiest of ways, though the breakage had, more than he anticipated, the effect of a crash. "For both of us?"

= But she shook, wonderfully, her head. "For either of us," she answered.

Page of Beerbohm manuscript pasted over a printed page of *A Christmas Garland*.

brownish-yellow. This is glue. Moisten slightly with water and attach to upper edge of printed vol.—page 9 of M.S. over page 9 of print; etcetera. (See Beerbohm's Hints to Bibliophiles.)" For a number of years I have wondered about those pages—where they were and what they said—to find them, of course, in the O'Connell Collection, dutifully pasted in Gosse's copy according to instructions. A small thing, no doubt, but very pleasant: an unpublished addition by the best parodist of his time to one of his best works in this genre.

Those author collections which were Mr. O'Connell's principal concern are as complete as he could make them, and subsidiary figures are admirably represented. It seems, for instance, as though everything published by John Lane must be here, not merely the books of his better-known writers. (Some readers may be surprised to learn that John Buchan was once published at the Bodley Head: *The Thirty-nine Steps* are a long way from Vigo Street, surely!) Two previous gifts of Mr. O'Connell to the Library, the major portions of his collections of Arthur Symons and of John Davidson—each containing letters and manuscripts—have now rejoined the main group.[2] Moreover, his Beardsley material is a most happy addition to the gift of the late A. E. Gallatin. Mr. Gallatin and Mr. O'Connell had divided between them a sizable correspondence addressed to the Beardsley family; these halves are now reunited to help form the outstanding Beardsley collection in the country.

For the most part Mr. O'Connell's books are in true Parrish condition, and it must be remembered that many of the colors selected for the cloth bindings were either fugitive or else so pale that they are easily soiled. Some volumes, like the purple-wrapped silver-lettered *Salomé* (1893), are fragile as well. It is therefore remarkable that so large a proportion of them are presentation copies; and when these are not inscribed by the author, they have some other and hardly less interesting association. Thus, Yeats's *Poems* (1895) was given to Gosse by

[2] See "John Davidson and Arthur Symons," *ibid.*, XV, No. 4 (Summer, 1954), 216-217.

Lionel Johnson, who wrote twelve lines of verse on the front flyleaf. Henley's *Song of the Sword* was Hardy's copy, with a few notes and markings in his hand. *The Child Set in the Midst*, containing Francis Thompson's first appearance in book form, was given by Wilfrid Meynell to John Drinkwater. Sir William Watson's *The Purple East* was inscribed to Clement Shorter by John Lane. H. De Vere Stacpoole's *Pierrot!* was given to Reginald Turner by Max Beerbohm.

There are a number of press books. At no point is the reaction to the taste of the previous generation so marked as in the physical appearance of books during the nineties. Shannon and Ricketts, who founded the Vale Press, decorated and illustrated books for John Lane and Leonard Smithers, the two publishers around whom this collection seems to revolve; and Beardsley created many binding designs as well as illustrations, as did Walter Crane. Kelmscott specimens are here, several being presentation copies from William Morris, and the Daniel and Ballantyne Presses are not forgotten.

Mr. O'Connell also secured a great many magazines of the period—not merely *The Yellow Book* and *The Savoy*, but less familiar and often shorter-lived publications: *The Butterfly, The Chameleon, The Albemarle, The Spirit Lamp, The Pageant, The Poster, The Century Guiid Hobby Horse, The Dome, The Quarto*—they are all here, even those numbers of *Kottabos* to which Wilde contributed when at Trinity College, Dublin.

Moreover, to remind us that there were other figures besides those of dandies and aesthetes, Mr. O'Connell compiled a small sampling of other contemporary writers, so that mingling with the company already described may be found such figures as Trilby, Sherlock Holmes, and Esther Waters, along with Mrs. Tanqueray and Mowgli, Liza of Lambeth and the Shropshire Lad.

What a richly varied decade it was! The past lingered on: Tennyson died in 1892, but Meredith and Swinburne lived into the twentieth century; Kipling achieved his reputation with his Indian tales as the decade opened, and by the time it was half over Hardy had abandoned fiction for poetry; Henry James's best work was still to come, although *Daisy Miller* had made him known as early as 1879. New names were crowding in (as Graham Robertson said, "Nobody was very old in the nineties."): Shaw published his first play in 1893, sandwiching it between the most entertaining musical and dramatic criticism in the language; within five years of that time Conrad, Wells, Galsworthy, and Bennett had each made his debut as a novelist. Yet we do not associate these people primarily with the era. It is unthinkable, for example, that any of them could ever have uttered Lionel Johnson's amiable warning to Le Gallienne when inviting him in for a nightcap: "I hope you drink absinthe, Le Gallienne; for I have nothing else to offer you." *There* is the keynote, to be echoed later by Enoch Soames: "Je me tiens toujours fidèle à la sorcière glauque." What characterized the period were those genuine but flickering and doomed talents, filled with a perversely conscious *diablerie*. Their reputations have suffered partial eclipse, but they still endure. If some of their gold leaf has peeled away, if some of the purple cloth has faded, the vellum hinges cracked, it is no great matter; we can discern beneath these things an ineffaceable impression of youthful fervor and discovery, and of youth's high hopes of excellence.

Bibliothecohimatiourgomachia

Our esteemed president should accept responsibility for this title; after all, he is an accomplished Grecian, which I am not. However, I will make a stab at translating it. We all remember Mr. Herman Liebert's stimulating paper at the January meeting, and with a bow in his direction I will render this majestic word in English as: "The importance of *not* having multiple copies."[1]

When Dr. Bühler trapped me into agreeing to make this talk I experienced the customary sinking sensation which overcomes me on such occasions. This time it was stronger than usual, because it recalled my first contact with the Bibliographical Society of America. Some years ago I mentioned to Carroll Wilson that I was collating the MS of a Trollope novel with the printed text. "Fine," he said, "will you let me have the result for the B.S.A. PAPERS?" The offer of so meteoric a rise to fame could not be rejected, and I hastened home to lard the article with footnotes and such scholarly apparatus as might render it fit for this Society. A week or two later I again encountered Carroll, who inquired about my progress. "Oh, I've nearly finished," I replied. Once more he said "Fine!" and then added the paralyzing injunction: "Make it funny." This appalling order produced in me a cataleptic condition from which I am still suffering.

And since I was reminded of Carroll, let me begin my talk by describing two of his books that are now in my possession. One is a copy of Trollope's *North America* presented by the author to an American friend. It had somehow strayed into a

---

Read at the meeting of the Bibliographical Society of America held on May 22, 1954, at Hartford, Connecticut, and printed in the Papers of the Society later that year.

[1] It may also be translated as "The Battle Between Libraries and Taylor."

New Hampshire public library, but had found its way out again, ending up in the hands of the bookseller who offered it to Carroll. Being a lawyer, he was not content until he had received from the librarian a quitclaim deed and a statement that the authorities were fully satisfied. This correspondence remains with the book, and shows clearly that because of the transaction the library was able to purchase material it greatly preferred. The second item is Hardy's *Dynasts*, including a copy of Part II with the 1905 title-page. This volume was found in the school library of Phillips Exeter Academy, and Carroll bought it from the trustees.

One other volume of mine that I wish to mention is a superb copy of Vaughan's *Silex Scintillans*, which was a Harvard duplicate. Here, then, are three books that I prize, and which I possess only because three very different libraries were willing and able to part with items which they did not really want. This behavior is not as common as you might think; and it is my contention that unless it becomes more general, the thwarted book collector of the next generation will be found amassing buttons or match-folders.

For desirable old books are disappearing from the market, and almost no collector is content merely to gather new books as they fall from the press. In all civilized ages the interest in collecting, whether of books or of other things, has been intensified by a desire to establish links with what has gone before. Books represent part of our inheritance of wisdom and beauty, and our ownership of them helps to assert our continuity with the past that produced them. No matter how modestly the collector starts, eventually he will come to seek some elusive rarity which by its age and perhaps by its association will communicate intimacy with some period or personality he admires. This same sentiment is shown by the pleasure most bookmen take in a volume with a distinguished provenance. I recently examined a book with an almost epic history: it was the Luttrell-Wynne-Heber-Utterson-Halliwell-Daniel-Huth-Clawson-Rosenbach copy. It has now found a good home—I know because I helped to send it there

—but its provenance has ended. At no time in the foreseeable future will any individual add his name to that impressive list.

Now the scholar will not regret this; in *Collector's Progress*[2] Mr. Wilmarth Lewis has admirably depicted the pitying scorn felt by a bibliographer for anyone who thought that a copy of *Bentley's Designs for Gray's Poems* could have any interest merely because it once belonged to Mrs. Vesey. Just the same, collectors *do* feel this way, and no amount of rational argument is going to change them. It must be clearly understood that, generally speaking, the collector is sentimental, illogical, selfish, romantic, extravagant, capricious; all the things, in fact, which the other three estates of the rare book world—scholars, dealers and librarians—cannot afford to be. It is true that these groups overlap. We all know people who belong in two, perhaps three, of these categories; but even so, their interest or career identifies them predominantly with only one. Our question at the moment is the importance of the collector to the other groups and to what extent they should pander to his vices.

He is by no means as necessary to the dealer as he once was; yet I submit that few dealers as yet would care to get along without him altogether. His relations with scholars are happier than they used to be. The old gibes on the one hand that the collector never read his books and on the other that the scholar did not know how to handle a fragile rarity are no longer heard. Each benefits freely from the other's activity. And as far as librarians are concerned, let me quote a sentence from *Lock, Stock and Barrel*, that history of collecting, by Douglas and Elizabeth Rigby.[3] ". . . it is a fact worthy of homage that most of the great libraries in the world, and most of the museums, were born in the homes of private collectors or have battened at the same source." That's the word they use: "battened." And Mr. John Carter has made some incisive observations on this point in his *Taste and Technique in Book-*

[2] New York, Alfred A. Knopf, 1951, p. 91.
[3] Philadelphia, J. B. Lippincott Company [1941], p. 82.

Collecting.[4] I quote him with especial pleasure, since you will all be glad to hear from him twice in one morning.

In America, the public-spirited tradition of Lenox and Brown has never died; and the impulse which moved Huntington and Folger, Clements and Chapin, to dignify their country, their state or their university with a monument worthily honoring their own names has of recent years been fortified by the activity of the tax-collector. Even of those many great collections which have been . . . dispersed by sale, some portions are always bought by or for institutional libraries. The number of desirable books, therefore, that are withdrawn from any reasonable possibility of further circulation becomes continually greater every year . . ."

And from the same volume:

There are more American critics than English of some of the present tendencies in American university library policy towards rare book-collecting . . . What is their concern is the growing volume of university buying in the rare book market, both public and private, which is the direct outcome of the greatly increased attention being paid to the rare book rooms on a hundred American campuses . . . Competition is a good thing in itself. But whether in the long run the rare book men in the university libraries can have it both ways is another matter. Bread sown on the waters in the shape of a liberal education in book-collecting to undergraduates may often return . . . But if the libraries all over a huge and wealthy continent are also going themselves to invade the auction rooms, the neglected parlors of stately homes, the file sets and MS cupboards of living writers and the various other sources normally tapped by collectors and the trade, it is conceivable that the time may come when they will drive their own pupils out of the market . . . Unless there is plenty of circulation bibliophily

[4] New York, R. R. Bowker Company, 1948.

cannot thrive; and the ultimate value of the bibliophile to pure scholarship as well as to the humanities of scholarship depends on his recognition as an active entity, not as a mere appendix.

A single instance will suffice to show what has been happening. I suppose no group of books is considered more generally desirable than the first editions of Shakespeare quartos. There are very few extant, as everyone knows; yet, between 1900 and 1939, fifty of them passed from private hands into American institutional libraries. It is likely that since then others have traveled the same road. Remember, I am speaking only of the first editions of the quartos—and I have not included any which were first published after 1622. These mournful statistics will not unduly depress realistic collectors; for a century it has been seldom that any individual aspired to collect Shakespeare in that manner, and now of course it is impossible. Not only is this true because there are practically no copies available, but because the price mounts with their scarcity. And the double effect on scarcity and price is symptomatic of what is happening to all rare books.

This, from the collector's point of view, is bad enough; but even worse is the duplication of holdings to be found in many institutions. These are generally the result of gifts or bequests —bequests so hedged about with threats and penalties, if any volume should be disposed of, that the librarian cannot release the duplicates. At least, not until a decent interval of time has elapsed. I have heard it said that in matters of testamentary disposition the word "forever" means "two years"; and I commend this idea to the study of librarians and their lawyers.

It is doubtless invidious to name any of these repositories of duplicates, but, as you would recognize them anyway, I may as well get on with it. Indeed, it is possible that all of our older libraries have duplicates which they may not part with, though I will limit myself to a few instances in the field of English literature. The New York Public Library, for example, has five copies of the First Folio. I don't know that the trustees would be especially eager to get rid of any of them, even if they could; still, once in a while those same trustees do try to raise money. And the Berg Collection in the same institution has two copies of *Tamerlane*, two of Bryant's *Embargo* in the original binding, two of Browning's *Pauline*, three of the Kilmarnock Burns, and six Pickwicks in parts. (The seventh copy lacks one part, so I pass over that.) Of course, unless work has been done on all these duplicates, it would be foolish to sell them; but after a careful examination has proved the extra copies to be identical, it would be equally foolish to keep them.

The Folger Library, as all the world knows, has a great number of Shakespeare Folios, which, with magnificent planning, were gathered together for the purpose of scholarship. At some time or other, all of them will have been collated and some will be found to be exact duplicates. It will be interesting to observe whether they will remain together just because it was once desirable to have them under one roof.

I do not know how many copies of *Paradise Lost* are essential to an institution's well-being; but the library of the University of Illinois has numerous copies of each issue, assembled for Professor Fletcher's monumental work.[5] Now that his work is published, the reason for that concentration has vanished—but there has been no rush to put any of the Illinois copies on the market. It is enough to make one question the value of state-supported education.

Let us turn to happier thoughts: the Huntington sales of duplicates, for instance. And of course even in these degenerate days there are occasional bright spots, as witness the three books with which I began this talk. And we must not forget the Pierpont Morgan Library, whose trustees have decided against the purchase of any printed rarity a copy of which is available in some other New York City institution. This deci-

---

[5] Harris Francis Fletcher, *ed.*, *John Milton's Complete Poetical Works Reproduced in Photographic Facsimile, A Critical Text Edition.* . . . Urbana, The University of Illinois Press, 1943-1948. 4 vols.

sion, I feel, is splendid. It comes a little late, perhaps, but there is more rejoicing in the collector's heaven over one sinner that repenteth than over the ninety-and-nine libraries that don't buy rare books. Such a policy will not enlarge the circulation which Mr. Carter mentions as necessary to bibliophily, but at any rate it will not decrease it.

To be sure, there exists a minimal circulation out of libraries: a book that seems to have found its final resting place *may* be moved. Very occasionally, a librarian will admit that a book under his charge might have a more suitable home elsewhere; and, less often, steps are actually taken to see that it does go elsewhere, rather like the bones of Napoleon being transferred from St. Helena to the Invalides. Under the circumstances, it is perhaps not surprising that "elsewhere" invariably means another institution.

But this is not constructive. Instead, let me urge on rare-book librarians, especially those whose institutions are comparative newcomers in the field, the following considerations:

1. That they make sure every item has a good reason for remaining on their shelves.
2. That all of them do not try to accumulate everything. Even Huntington limited himself to three areas, and it is no longer possible to collect on the scale that he did.
3. That when their fields are decided on, they make the library's aims known to present and potential benefactors.
4. That they explain to such benefactors the hampering nature of gifts or bequests with elaborate restrictions—and, if needful, have the courage to refuse them. It might be useful to suggest to some donors that their books could be sold for the benefit of the library; and, if they are seeking some form of immortality, to remind them that the names of Britwell, Huth and Clawson are probably better known in the book world than those of Spencer, Coe and Parrish. Often the name on an auction catalogue endures as well as though it were carved on a lintel; and the sale price of a collection would benefit many a library more than would the collection itself.
5. And finally, that each librarian whose institution is in any way

dependent upon individual benefactors ask himself whether those individuals would be as helpful if none of them were collectors.

It is the libraries who now have the whip hand, and who can determine, in these days of increasing socialism, how far private enterprise in this field is to be encouraged. For the collecting streams are being fished out, and they will have to be restocked somehow if collecting is to continue as it has in the past. I am well aware that this is a venerable complaint. Nearly every collector has at some point moaned that he will never be able to get any really important books. Certainly we need go back no further than Harry Elkins Widener, who, according to A. E. Newton, lamented, "Mr. Morgan and Mr. Huntington are buying up all the books, and Mr. Bixby is getting the manuscripts. When my time comes—if it ever does—there will be nothing left for me—everything will be gone!"[6] Our grief at this outcry can be mitigated by recalling that he did manage to secure the Van Antwerp First Folio, the Countess of Pembroke's copy of the *Arcadia*, the dedication copy of Boswell's *Life of Johnson*, and many similar items.

Nevertheless, I repeat that wail, familiar as it may be. Books are being absorbed by institutions at a greater rate than ever before, and the pace seems always to accelerate. Mr. Wilmarth Lewis does not think that the Farmington Plan will be used in this field. "It is too much to expect," he says, "that libraries will transfer their rariora in any wholesale manner." Yet eventually what other solution will there be? The number of demands continues to increase. The Davison books have gone to Wesleyan, the Lewis to Texas Christian, and the Philips—or perhaps I should say the Wilmerding—to Haverford. In at least two of these places accommodation had to be built especially to receive the collections, showing that these colleges had not previously contemplated this type of acquisition. And at least two of them have promised that their new

[6] A. Edward Newton, *The Amenities of Book-Collecting and Kindred Affections* (Boston, The Atlantic Monthly Press [c1918]), p. 352.

rare bookrooms will not be mere showcases, but will be centers for study as well as for further accumulation. Truly, of buying many books there is no end—or of plans for buying them, anyway. Robert Hoe's query has more significance for these times than it did for his own: "If the great libraries of the past had not been sold, where would I have found my books?" And where will the libraries find them now? But answer, as the poet observes, came there none; and this was scarcely odd, because they'd eaten every one.

If by any chance anyone present should think that this disquisition has appeared slightly biased, that it has not seemed purely objective, he would be quite right. But do not think that I contemplate spoiling the Egyptians. It is impossible to overestimate the value of the great institutional libraries that enrich this country; and the fact that many of them were created in the last fifty years is a tribute to the foresight and generosity of the past generation, and to the energy and skill of those who have followed. I myself shall always be grateful for the many kindnesses shown me by librarians and for the friendships I have made among them. At least, they were my friends up till now. But whether or not they have begun to regard me with suspicion, I am certain they will agree with a dealer who was irritated by some remark I once made in the course of an argument. "The trouble with you," he said, turning on me bitterly, "the trouble with you is that you're just like every other God-damned collector." And, ladies and gentlemen, I don't ask for any better tribute.

The Common Habitation

The honor of being asked to address you, gentlemen, is a rather overpowering one; and after some diligent searching, I find that the only topic about which I know more than you do is—myself. It is not, perhaps, a very inspiring one; but after all, the reason I am here tonight is merely that I am a book-collector, so that we may as well examine the nature of that curiously-constituted animal.

I have said elsewhere that "generally speaking, the collector is sentimental, illogical, selfish, romantic, extravagant, capricious—all the things, in fact, which the other three estates of the rare book world—scholars, dealers, and librarians—cannot afford to be." Dealers and librarians are of necessity brought into contact with collectors, and it will be well if the scholars —you, gentlemen—also know something of this frivolous dilettante. How did he start on his downward path?

Well, in my case it happened quite simply: a series of illnesses in childhood developed a habit of reading, reading entirely for pleasure, without any sordid wish to learn anything or improve the mind. There never seemed to be enough books around, and what I priggishly wanted at home was a library. You may recall Emerson's warning to the young: "Be careful what you wish for: you may get it." I have a library now; and I've brought down here a few things from it which you may care to look at later. I have described the collection and a little of its history in an article that appeared some years ago in the *Book Collector*; if anyone here happens to have encountered this, I apologize for the repetition.

It was during my last year in prep school that I discovered old books. The period was only a few years before 1929, when

This address was delivered at the Princeton Graduate College on April 19, 1957 to the graduate students in English and members of the English Faculty.

prices reached an all time high. It was a perilous time in which to buy anything desirable, and, naturally, impossible to do so on a schoolboy's allowance. I decided (since I would never be able to afford a first edition) to try to get what I thought of as "contemporary" editions of the books I wanted. The first item I bought was an eighth edition of Johnson's *Lives of the Poets*; being more blasé now, I find it difficult to convey to you with what an excitement, as of one entering the portals of the past, I read those volumes of 1794. And just about the time when the Jerome Kern copy of *Robinson Crusoe* (the first edition, 1719, in contemporary calf) was fetching $11,500 at auction I was spending my little all on a rebound copy of the Stockdale edition of 1790. It was not quite the same thing, but it *was* an eighteenth-century edition, with long esses just as they should be, and it seemed to me infinitely preferable to any nineteenth- or twentieth-century reprint.

As a matter of fact, it still does. The "flavor of the period" is not a meaningless phrase, and even at such removes as I have mentioned it has a certain force. Our only difficulty in reading things of earlier eras is to relate them to our times as well as their own; and anything, no matter how slight, that provides helpful links in the chain is of value. You may consider this to be part of the sentimentality to which I referred a moment ago. In a more extreme form it has been well described by Sir Max Beerbohm, who says:

> After all, the reason (I had almost said, the excuse) for desiring first editions of an author whose work one likes is that they give one a sense of nearness to him . . . 'This is the binding *he* chose—perhaps. This—perhaps—is the fount of type that *he* insisted on. Here certainly is a typographical error that *his* eye overlooked—bless his noble spirit!'

Yet in spite of the ridicule this dreamy attitude finds a basis in fact. Everything, including books and ideas, is in a furious race with oblivion; and by clutching more firmly these relics of previous times we feel that we can help save them from being washed away by Lethe. Knowledge must be learned over again by each generation, and, as I have just said, the task is simpler when some kind of assistance is available to demonstrate our own continuity with the past. This is not merely the fancy of a collector trying to justify his whims. Listen to Mr. Robert Birley, the Headmaster of Eton, talking about the rare books in that college's library: "Eton, you will say, is a school and not a university. Well, we live at a time when the cry is all for Visual Aids in education. I have yet to find a visual aid more satisfactory than a good library of old books." And he is, happily for scholars of the next generation, not alone in his belief.

But to return to my own collecting. I liked to read Trollope, and no definitive edition of his work was ever issued. The only certain way to assemble a reading set was, and still is, to buy first editions. I had no ambition to become a Trollope collector, you must realize; if I could have found a reasonably complete set I would have been quite content. But I bought whatever battered copies came to hand, the cheaper the better, thinking that one day I might be able to afford a uniform binding for them. Before this could happen, I acquired one book, *The Last Chronicle of Barset*, whose condition was too good to permit rebinding. This item eventually upset the whole applecart: it made me dissatisfied with the others, and eventually I began to replace them.

Every good collector, of course, should have a plan. I did not know this—indeed, I do not seem to have known anything—and there came a day when I was tempted to branch out. By any system of logic, I should have progressed to another Victorian novelist; but what tempted me was two books, neither having anything to do with Trollope. They were both presentation copies: Browning's *Paracelsus* and the 1834 *Sartor Resartus*. From that time on I was lost. There came certain Americans—*Moby Dick, Huckleberry Finn, Two Years Before the Mast*—interspersed with *The Rivals*, Pepys' *Diary*, and the 1645 Milton's *Poems*; there was no order, no reason, no sanity, except that I wanted each volume, and the sanity of that may well have been open to question.

As time passed, the malady raged like the measles in Samoa. Letters were added, and a few manuscripts. But no collector is ever really satisfied with what he has. I reflect occasionally on the large number of books without which I can never really be happy, and which I shall never have even a chance to buy—and none of which could I possibly afford in any case. This, you will observe, is exactly the frame of mind in which I started. But it is commonly a part of the disease. Thomas Baker, the seventeenth-century collector, complained that "the men of quality lay out so much for books, and give such high prices, that there is nothing left for poor scholars." It was as much as he could do, he said, "to pick up a few at tolerable prices, and despair of any more." Dibden moaned that "books grow scarcer every day"—and that was very nearly a hundred and fifty years ago.

For collectors tend to be more conscious of the gaps on their shelves than of the books. Especially is this true of the gaps that might have been filled: the book that one felt would be an extravagance—until it was sold to someone else; the book that wasn't quite fine enough—except that no other copy has turned up since; the book that one didn't take because of ignorance, and which one may never see again. There was a beautiful inscribed copy of *Bells and Pomegranates* about which I dallied too long; the copy of *Salomé* that Wilde gave to Robert Ross after it had been decorated with caricatures by Beerbohm and Charles Ricketts—a luckier collector found it before I did; the *Moll Flanders*, for which a dreadful price was asked. It is always the lost sheep that concern us, not those safely in the fold.

However, in the midst of these losses I did acquire a number of items, enough so that when I began finally to evolve a plan for the collection, there was nothing it could be except English and American literature. It could never be more than a skeletonic arrangement, but I trusted that all the principal authors and periods would be represented, if only sketchily. When I bought *The Lives of the Poets*, nothing could have been farther from my thoughts; but this grandiose scheme was forced upon me by the books I had already acquired. They now range from half-a-dozen manuscripts of the fifteenth century—Wyclif, Higden's *Polychronicon*, Lydgate, Gower, and so on—to fairly complete runs of some of the Bloomsbury group: E. M. Forster, Virginia Woolf, and Lytton Strachey. Plus the gaps, naturally; an endless series of them. This is not exactly keeping the collection up to date, of course; but the effort of trying to span, with however flimsy a bridge, five hundred years of English literature is strain enough.

At this point some of you may be reminded of one of Christopher Morley's *Translations from the Chinese*:

> And while my visitor prattled
> I courteously nodded;
> My eye was fast upon him,
> My face bright with attention;
> But inwardly I was saying:
> "The excellent fellow, why does he tell me all this?
> What has it to do with me?
> O Buddha, when will he depart?"

Well, it has this to do with you: that in your work there cannot be too close an association with original texts and, where possible, author's manuscripts. Of course much work must be done with the aid of photostat and microfilm, but this is at the best a substitute for the genuine article. A. E. Newton compared it to kissing a girl through a sheet of plate glass. Mr. Liebert of the Yale Library told me that a historian had once deprecated to him the vast sums spent on building up Yale's manuscript holdings. "Microfilm would be just as good," he said. To which Mr. Liebert responded, "Very well. Your field is seventeenth-century English history. Let us suppose that a hitherto unknown letter from Oliver Cromwell comes to light, announcing his firm resolve to make himself King. This item upsets all our previous ideas of Cromwell, so you obtain a microfilm of it and produce a scholarly monograph on the subject. Three days after it appears in print, you learn that the paper of this document is watermarked 1811. What do you do then?" This may be an extreme hypothesis, but there are enough pitfalls in the wilderness of scholarship without adding to them unnecessarily. Let us take it for granted as an axiom that no scholar can really master his subject unless he is familiar with contemporary editions and documents.

Without putting myself in the exalted company of scholars, let me tell you about a Charlotte Brontë letter I once had. The signature was the rare "C. Nichols," and though the letter itself didn't look altogether like the few letters I had then seen, who was I to dispute its authenticity with the dealer who sold it to me? To cut a long story short, it is now in the New York Public Library's collection of forgeries. But the point is that I don't believe that I would be fooled by a similar item today; and this (perhaps unjustified) confidence is due, not to any exhaustive study, but simply to careful examination of those specimens which I have since had the opportunity to see.

This kind of familiarity is very useful; not only for the valuable hunches it may give you when dealing with complete documents, but also when you are dealing with uncatalogued or defective material. Would I do as well as I hope I might with an unsigned, undated fragment of a Brontë letter? There exist many mutilated letters of all periods: the autograph hounds of past generations were very busy with their scissors. They are now all frizzling in hell; certainly we trust that their barbarous activity is no longer practiced. But often we must deal with what they left us, or with material which has been damaged accidentally. If possible, it must somehow be made to tell you more than the mere words it carries.

There is also bibliography, in the last few decades an increasingly recognized tool of textual scholarship. And that can be pursued only with original editions; no facsimiles or reprints will help you here.

Indeed, the mere matter of choosing a text to read is by no means as simple as might be thought. You are probably aware that Henry James would publish the same story in somewhat

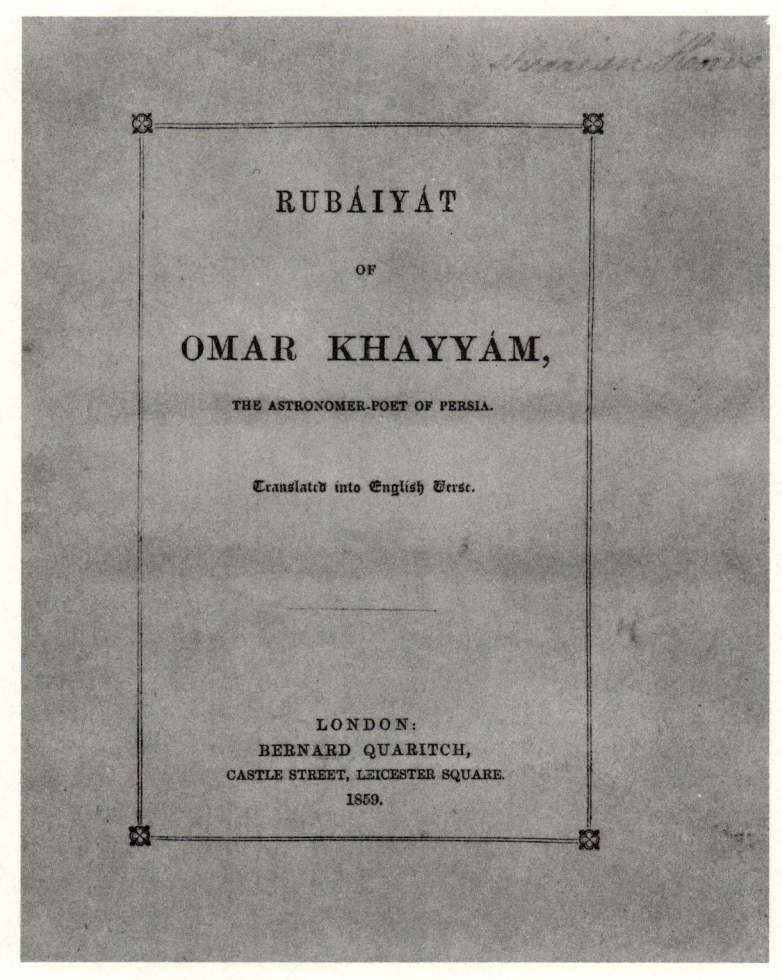

First edition of Fitzgerald's *Rubáiyát* of Omar Khayyám.

different versions in magazines both here and in England. He would then re-write it when it appeared in book form in both countries. And that inveterate reviser would again alter it for the Scribner edition of his collected works. Which is correct—the early, fresh version or the late one, irridescent with subtlety? What are you to do—unless, like Leon Edel, you read them all? The ordinary reader, fortunately for his reason, is spared this knowledge, but you are not; and you cannot argue about the details of, say, *Roderick Hudson* as set forth in the New York edition with someone who clings to the earliest text.

Second thoughts are not always improvements. The hundreds of editions of Rubáiyát (which mushroomed when the poem began to be popular) are almost without exception reprints of the fourth edition. Much new material appears for the first time in that version; but Fitzgerald, tinkering with the older stanzas, seems progressively to remove the poetry from them. Here is the first stanza in its first form:

> Awake! for Morning in the Bowl of Night
> Has flung the Stone that puts the Stars to Flight:
> And Lo! the Hunter of the East has caught
> The Sultan's Turret in a Noose of Light.

And this is the final reading:

> Wake! for the Sun who scatter'd into flight
> The Stars before him from the Field of Night,
> Drives Night along with them from Heav'n, and strikes
> The Sultan's Turret with a Shaft of Light.

How very flat and inferior to the first one!

There is the matter of nineteenth-century American editions of contemporary English books. They are not always to be trusted. They were for the most part pirated, and the author never had a chance to correct the proofs. Often there was a race to get the books on the market, and in consequence they were carelessly produced. An extreme case was that of Scott. He wrote rapidly, and made nearly all of his corrections and emendations on the proof-sheets, rather than his manuscript. The story goes that some enterprising American bribed the foreman of Ballantyne's press to rush an early set of proofs to the fastest packet sailing for America; and so certain American editions, set up from uncorrected proofs and containing all Scott's errors and slips, were issued here almost as soon as the approved text appeared in Edinburgh.

Then, too, there is the well-established but erroneous notion that a modern text published by a reputable press must be correct. In this connection, let me recount a little story about a distinguished Englishman. He is an extremely eminent scholar, and in his later years he has enjoyed playing a game of his own devising. Reading a favorite author, he will decide that such-and-such a phrase was mangled by the printer, for it does not sound quite like the style of the work—and this scholar knows the styles of his favorites very well indeed. He will then proceed to divine what the author intended to say, and publish the result. Having attained a kind of scholastic Nirvana, he does not feel any need to compare his guesses with an earlier source. The editor of a journal to whom an article of his was once offered asked me to check it against the manuscript, which was in New York. Our scholar had based his "hariolations," as he called them, on a modern edition issued by a famous press, and he blithely observed at the start that "serious errors in [this edition] are improbable." But when I collated his article with the manuscript and a copy of the first edition, I found that nearly half of the errors, for which he has a fabulously sharp eye, occurred in this modern edition and there only. The craftsmen whom A. E. Housman called "those beasts of printers" have always been fallible, like the rest of us.

All of the foregoing is an effort to persuade you to as close contact as possible with original material, and one of the pleasantest ways of establishing such contact is to collect. Admittedly, for this one needs, among other things, opportunity. During my undergraduate days there was a branch of the

Brick Row Bookshop on Nassau Street; it disappeared in the depression, but while it lasted it offered the agreeable experience of poring over the stock, complaining loudly of the prices, and comparing both of them with the catalogues of other establishments. I regret that you do not have a chance now to squander time, if not money, in a similar spot.

And, speaking of money, all the treatises on collecting for beginners will tell you that you need hardly any. This is comforting, and even, to a very slight extent, true; but then you must be willing to stick to minor or out-of-the-way authors, not earlier than the eighteenth century. I say "authors" rather than "subjects" because your field is literature. However, even these minor uncollected authors are getting harder to find, and many English ones, such as Constance Holme or Winwood Reade, are not easily met with in American bookshops. The determined collector will find his own way around such difficulties. In the first volume of the *Book Collector* there is a most interesting account by J. C. T. Oates, of the Cambridge University Library, of his Sterne collection. It contains no first edition of *Tristram Shandy* or *A Sentimental Journey*, but more can be learned from it about Sterne and his popularity than those two expensive items can ever tell us. Currently unfashionable authors are an excellent choice; when Michael Sadleir began his collecting, Trollope and Melville languished forgotten on dealers' shelves. But remember: you must like and believe in the value of what you collect, or your interest will die a-borning.

One reason so much material today is scarce and expensive is the tremendous amount garnered in the last few decades by American institutional libraries. I have publicly delivered an anathema against their activities, and have no intention of repeating it here. Suffice it to say that they interfere seriously with my own program. And since life is full of conflicts, I also find myself a member of the Princeton Library's Advisory Council and Chairman of the Friends of the Library. This dichotomy has induced a certain schizophrenia; you will understand, therefore, that while on the one hand I deplore the piling up of valuable books by these unfeeling, soulless institutions, on the other I am obliged to persuade everyone to take an active interest in Princeton's holdings, and do whatever is possible to improve them.

Mention of the Library brings up one more topic: the relation of the collector to the institution. Every institutional library of any consequence anywhere in the world owes its origin or at any rate its eminence to the private collector. In the last few generations the American collector has come to realize, sometimes with a slight pang, that his books will eventually be lodged in an institution, whether he himself donates them or not. He has been only their temporary custodian. He and others like him have cared for the books until the institution, so to speak, was ready to receive them. He perhaps even fancied himself a link connecting the author and the librarian; and if he had gleefully read the late Randolph Adams' *Librarians as Enemies of Books* he would certainly have felt himself akin to Vishnu the Preserver standing between Brahma the Creator and Siva the Destroyer.

Now that the great days of Morgan and Huntington are over, however, there is another and friendlier relation. No one today can amass treasures on so imperial a scale, but libraries still rely on individuals for assistance and gifts and, above all, intelligent cooperation. It would be difficult to overestimate the value of Mr. Wilmarth Lewis to Yale, for example, or Mr. Waller Barrett to Virginia, and they are only two among many. This tie is a favorable portent for the future of American scholarship.

In the field you have chosen much of your work will be done in libraries. I earnestly urge upon you the necessity for getting on friendly terms immediately with the librarian, wherever your work may call you. Try to understand his problems. You may even be able to help him with some of them; certainly he will be in a position to help you with some of yours. He is a collector, of course, though not necessarily a private one. He cannot afford to buy everything his library should have; and if you are in a position to convince him that the material you need is too important to miss—why, so much the better for you. If you are familiar with collecting difficulties you will more easily establish a bond of sympathy; and if you can interest collectors in your institution, you will confer a great potential benefit upon it. To do this you must understand and enter into their enthusiasms. Such understanding is partly a matter of temperament: not all of you may be sympathetic to their craving for the physical possession of desiderata. But at least you can understand the reason for this craving: it is, among other things, the tribute they pay to the prized achievement of the past.

The tribute is not less sincere than yours because of the form it takes. A true collector is as familiar with the merits of his books as he is with their commercial value. The ancient slander that he knows only their exteriors is most certainly untrue today. Indeed, gentlemen, the reason we are together in this room tonight is because we love the English language and the rich and varied excellence of its literature. That is the common habitation of scholars and collectors alike—a habitation compounded, as Sir Henry Wotton declared all good architecture to be, of firmness, commodity, and delight.

II

THE WRITER'S CRAFT

Authors at Work

It has been a number of years since a member of the Arrangements Committee addressed the Club, and when I was first considering this talk I thought you might like to hear about the work that such an exhibition involves. A long dissertation could be made on this theme: locating the material, negotiating the loan of it ("Shut not your doors to *me*, proud libraries!"), setting it in place, writing labels, and so on. The crises are frequent: the owner of some essential and unique item has already agreed to lend it elsewhere; the trustees of some library, who must approve all its loans, will not meet again until the day after our show is to open; an individual who months ago promised desirable material has suddenly gone abroad without warning. There is the valuable book or document which disappears ("It must be here *somewhere*; have you looked through all that wrapping-paper?"). Well, it turns up; at least, in my experience it has always done so. But at times my experience has been rather unnerving.

Quite as bad is the fear, always present to anyone working on a show, that some item will be damaged. The Club keeps a half-hearted file of documents relating to its exhibitions, and when working on my first show here I consulted it. In the course of doing so, I ran across an unfinished, unsigned draft of a letter to Morris L. Parrish. "Dear Mr. Parrish," it began, "I hardly know how to tell you this; but during the work of setting up the exhibit, Volume One of your copy of *Desperate Remedies* fell from the shelf, breaking its spine. I do not know what to" . . . that was all. The handwriting was unknown to me, and I could only conclude that the writer had taken

This address was delivered at the opening of an exhibition of literary manuscripts at the Grolier Club on October 18, 1955. The Club published it in 1957.

the easy way out—i.e., instead of finishing the letter he had gone home and cut his throat.

Anecdotes of that kind could be multiplied indefinitely. But tonight we are surrounded by manifestations of the creative spirit at work, and it will be more profitable to turn our attention to the contents of the cases.

First of all I would like to point out that very few of the exhibits are the sort of draft the ordinary man would produce. Almost every one of them shows unmistakable signs of the most intense concentration, whether the author is wrestling with ideas, vast piles of research material, or merely a resistant medium, like the Russian language. Only the fiercely determined writer can conquer interruptions—the person from Porlock who calls on business—without losing the continuity of his work. Sir Alan Herbert once described quite vividly what I mean, and I will quote practically all of his article:

> Copies of the original manuscript of Mr. Arnold Bennett's *The Old Wives' Tale* have been published at a high figure. They are worth it. I have been privileged to see the original, and it is *the* wonder of the world. So neat, so precise, so rarely marred by erasure or alteration, so beautiful, it is more like a priest's copy of a traditional religious work than the original record of a creative masterpiece. I have recently referred to some of my own old manuscripts, and I find them equally remarkable, but for different reasons. Not only did Mr. Bennett know exactly what he wanted to say and how he was going to say it; but it seems that while he wrote the book no one rang him up and left messages, no one called about the rates, no one made it necessary for him to do elaborate sums or draw pictures or diagrams; and no other masterpieces occurred to him while he was at work upon *The Old Wives' Tale*. Moreover, he wrote legibly in ink, and in prose; I write a sort of intoxicated shorthand, in pencil. I have found a few fragments in old notebooks which make it clear that Mr. Bennett's method is quite different from my own. For instance, here is a page or two

taken at random from the manuscript of the poem "I like them fluffy":

        Some like them little and sweet
                        proud
        Some like them tall and severe
        Sme like them stuffed with conceit
        And To some the shy virgin is dear
                  damsel

huffy And some of the   love the whole crowd

        But I like them fluffy I freely conf
        With eyes that are like   a pretty blue dress

   Victoria 7203
           Tell Gwen the aunts
           will come to tea

     With fluffy soft cheeks
         Like plums on a wall
     And what I may call

     I like them fluffy   A fluffy soft heart
         With no brains   And no brains at all

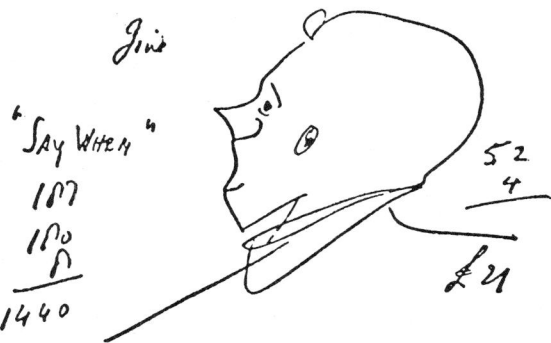

> Brains are all right in their place
> > But I find it

You are a leader writer on *The Daily Herald*. Write a short leading article of not more than 300 words entitled "Autumn" and leading up logically to an appeal for the nationalization of the means of production distrib   and exc

> Chiswick 2710
> > I will be Bohemian I will

> Can Lavender have tea with the Rowntrees?
> > Don't let's go to the dogs tonight
> > > For mother will be there

> Some like a girl
> > Who cares if the charmer's well-read   red
> > > the Society

> And some like a shingle or crop
> > But I don't care what
> Who cares what she's got in her head
> > If she's plenty of hair on the top?

Alas! that so many one meets

> > Tell Gwen the *geyser*

Brains are all right in their plac

> > 24 Upper Cheyne Row

Better be broke by a blonde
> Than bored by a brainy brunette

    Brains are all right in their place   <u>PAY</u>
     But oh what a shock to the heart   <u>GAS</u>
      If a lady   embrace
        To express her   Art
        To enquire
    Or is constantly giving her views
     On a Czecho-Slovakian play
And today as I paused on t   brink
              annoyed
  She sighed and said 'What do you think

           FREUD

Park 8075   Trout   *Friday* w'out fail

   Not huffy not stuffy not tiny or tall
   But fluffy just fluffy with no brains
    I like them fluffy I gently replied

Mortimers will be there 4.30 but can you bring a racquet they can't come to supper thank god

   with downy soft eyebrows and artful blue eyes
        highbrows   despise

$$\frac{5000 \times \overset{5}{60}}{12} \qquad 2500$$

$$\frac{20/2500}{125}$$

$$\frac{125 \times 10}{100} \qquad \pounds 125 \times 12$$

       <u>INSURANCE</u>
  I wish I was horribly rich

With fluffy complexion like plums on a wall
And   at all
   I will be Bohemian I swear
   But I should like a breath of fresh air

There must, I suppose, have been other stages before the final draft was reached, but they will never be published, for I cannot find them. There *was* a final version, I know, but how much less exciting!

Now that is the kind of manuscript that we might produce ourselves—if we had a brilliant flair for witty verse. But these exhibits are different: different from each other as well as from this. They show varying methods of approach, they depend in varying degree on inspiration and re-writing. They *are* more exciting than what was eventually published, it is true; that is partly because the unfinished has a certain appeal to the imagination. As Sir Max Beerbohm said, "Mr. Pickwick and the Ancient Mariner are valued friends of ours, but they do not preoccupy us like Edwin Drood or Kubla Khan." And there is also a sentimental aspect of the appeal which these exhibits have for us: they are closer to the author. A fanciful person may even visualize the authors busily scribbling; their instruments vary, of course: goose-quills, steel pens, lead pencils—surely Ouida can have used nothing less than an ostrich plume—while from one corner comes the faint clack of typewriters. But their purpose is the same, and the way in which these manuscripts are written will tell us much about their authors.

Pope, for example: he said of himself that as a child he "lisped in numbers, for the numbers came." If so, they soon ceased to come readily; that indication of facility is denied altogether by those drafts of the *Essay on Man*. His avowed aim was correctness, the ideal of his time, and we see that he spared nothing to achieve it. But that rather frigid ambition does not entirely explain his laborious scrawls. We must remember that Pope was the first English writer to make a fortune by his writings alone, and that the early eighteenth century admired, respected and rewarded literary excellence as no other age has done before or since. Prior, Congreve, Addison and Steele were all given government positions because they wrote well. Pope wrote well also, but was debarred from such favors by his Catholicism. However, he may have received as much as £9000 for his translation of Homer (the exact amount is unknown), and this sum must be reckoned as over two hundred thousand dollars today. His popularity was absolute; as always in such a case, there were temptations to alter his standards. He was offered bribes to mention people favorably, and refused them. He did accept £1000 from the Duchess of Marlborough to suppress a satire on the Duke—and he then proceeded to publish a scathing description of the Duchess herself. It is true, of course, that Pope seldom mentioned anyone favorably; indeed, Lytton Strachey described Pope's theme as "civilization illumined by animosity; such was the passionate and complicated material from which he wove his patterns of balanced precision and polished clarity." But out of what chaos did that clarity and precision come! His effort to clothe his thoughts in the smoothest possible verse was, as you may see, enormous; and not even the spur of his many hatreds could be allowed to hasten his labors, even though the success of whatever he published was assured in advance.

The School for Scandal presents the opposite situation. Ideas came to Sheridan faster than he could set them down. An early draft, which is called simply *Sir Peter Teazle*, starts out as a routine comedy of the period on the theme of the elderly husband and the young wife. The play commences with a long soliloquy by Sir Peter (who has retired from trade) about his marital misfortunes—and then something happens. The characters come to life so rapidly that Sheridan has no time even to indicate which one is speaking; references to unwritten scenes are jotted down on blank pages; the whole thing expands under our eyes. Although the scandalmongers who ultimately provided the play with its title are not mentioned in the dialogue, they begin, none the less, to exist in Sheridan's mind. On an otherwise empty page is the notation "Crabtree to wear a Muff"—and that is all we hear of him until the final version. Again, we find the isolated words "Lady

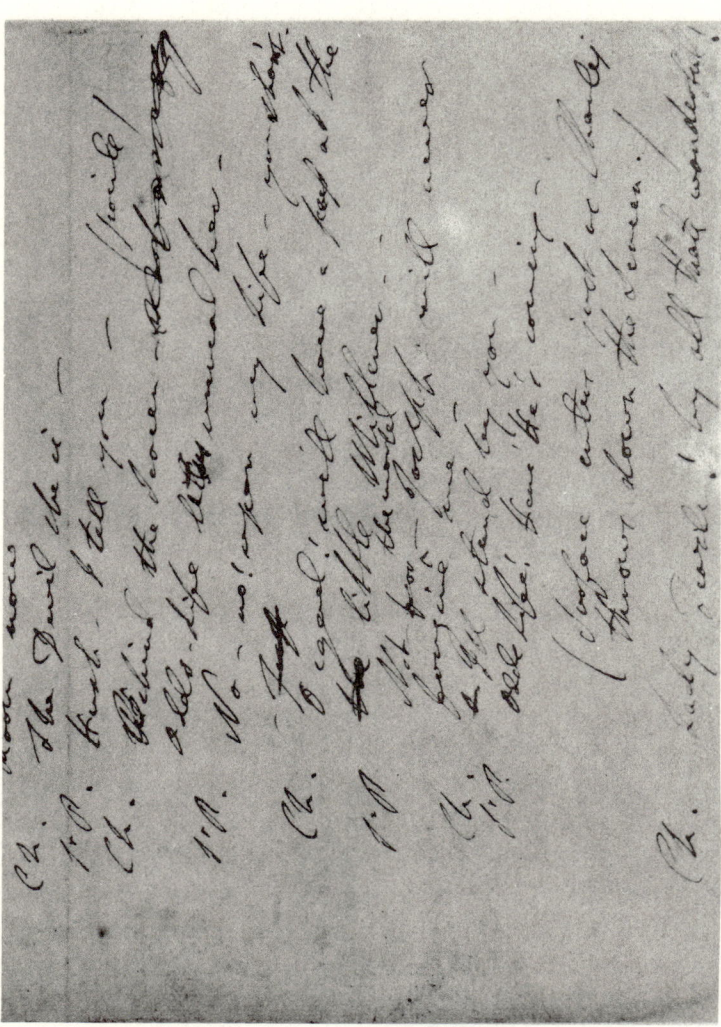

The beginning of the "screen scene" in Sheridan's manuscript of *The School for Scandal*.

Sneerwell to be with Joseph"—and that lady, who begins the play in its final form, is not spoken of elsewhere. And, at the top of one of the last pages, in Sheridan's own form of abbreviation, is the phrase "Sk for Sk."

His speed in composition was attested by many of his contemporaries. Michael Kelly, associated with him at Drury Lane, was commissioned to compose the music for Sheridan's tragedy *Pizaro*. He tells how Sheridan failed to send him the words of the songs until a very few days before the performance, and continues:

> But if this were a puzzling situation for a composer, what will my readers think of that in which the actors were left, when I state the fact that, at the time the house was overflowing with people on the first night's performance, all that was written of the play was actually rehearsing; and that, incredible as it may seem, until the end of the fourth act neither Mrs. Siddons, nor Charles Kemble, nor Barrymore had all their speeches for the fifth? Mr. Sheridan was upstairs in the prompter's room where he was writing the last part of the play, while the earlier parts were acting; and every ten minutes he brought down as much of the dialogue as he had done, into the green-room, abusing himself and his negligence, and making a thousand winning and soothing apologies, for having kept the performers so long and in such painful suspense.

Reliance on last-minute inspiration could be carried no further, and after *Pizaro* Sheridan attempted nothing more for the theater.

Dickens was another writer with deadlines to meet; but his superabundant energy would not permit him such lazy procrastination. Indeed, he could not get physically tired by sitting at a desk. He wrote so many letters (about ten thousand have survived) that one wonders how he was able to produce any novels at all. Yet when he described to Professor Felton the composition of *A Christmas Carol*, he said that

> he wept and laughed and wept again, and excited himself in a most extraordinary manner in the composition; and thinking whereof he walked about the black streets of London, fifteen and twenty miles many a night when all the sober folk had gone to bed. . . . Its success is most prodigious. And by every post all manner of strangers write all manner of letters to him about their homes and hearths, and how this same Carol is read aloud there, and kept on a little shelf by itself.

Dicken's passion for strenuous walking—his letters are full of it—is well-known; and though many authors have paced the floor in the throes of composition, very few have traveled as far as twenty miles a night in the process. And of course, after all this pedestrianism, though the story was clearly laid out in his mind, the book remained to be written,—and rewritten, as the manuscript shows. Every page of it is scored all through with corrections, yet its gusto and exuberance are as fresh as though it had been set down without alteration.

An example of the meticulous artist at work may be seen in the page here displayed of Tennyson's *Maud*. As early as 1832 he was writing to publisher Moxon:

> I think it would be better to send me every proof twice over—I should like the text to be as correct as possible—to be sure this would somewhat delay the publication, but I am in no hurry. My manuscripts (i.e., those I have by me) are far from being in proper order and such a measure would both give me leisure to arrange and collect them and ensure a correct type. I scarcely know at present what the size of the volume will be, for I have many poems lying by me with respect to which I cannot make up my mind as to whether they are fit for publication . . . if such be the case and you send me every proof twice how long would your printer be in getting the book ready?

He was in no hurry, not he! And he never ceased making alterations, before, during and after publication.

Mr. John Collier, in a penetrating essay on Tennyson, observes that he

> had not a subtle but a supersubtle sense of words. In one respect his best lines exceed Shakespeare's: they have more iris to them. It is better to have written "It is a nipping and an eager air" or "The dawn in russet mantle clad" than
>
> "walk'd in a wintry wind in a ghastly glimmer and found
> The shining daffodil dead, and Orion low in his grave."
>
> But it is Tennyson's couplet which is palpitating and phosphorescent, almost corrupt, with consciousness and sensibility. It is unwholesome to be as venison-ripe as this, but it is very lovely, don't you think? And, closer to our point, he who made that unerring stroke, that exquisite lie, *shining*, never set down word numbly or unknowingly.

Yet, as the manuscript discloses, "unerring" is not exactly the right epithet. Tennyson made at least three shots before he achieved that target, and had already gathered a whole wreath of sweet narcissus and golden aconite when he finally decided on the daffodil.

Now this constant revision on Tennyson's part was due largely to the wish (shared by so many other authors) to see his work in what he called "correct type." But there is one poet represented in the exhibit who, after a single timid inquiry, abandoned all thought of publication: Emily Dickinson. I need not relate again the story of the Amherst recluse, writing in secret, occasionally sending a poem to a friend or relative; but it is surely appropriate to state once more the platitude that not only is the advent of genius mysterious but that so little may cause it to germinate. Her home, its garden, its orchard, a shadowy and unrequited love—these were sufficient to make her one of the great lyricists of all literature. Mr. Thomas Johnson's edition of her complete poems enables us to examine them at last free from editorial changes, and it emphasizes one particular facet of her method. During her lifetime the great bulk of her poetry was never seen by anyone else, and this composing for herself in solitude was both a strength and a weakness. In the poem shown here, *One need not be a chamber*, there is evidence of revision and improvement; but this did not always occur. Ludwig Lewisohn pointed out years ago that

> a note for a poem served her as well as a poem, and that when either the rhyme that marked artistic completion did not come to her, or the lyric logic refused to unfold itself harmoniously, she was quite or almost as happy as in the contrary case. In a word, the very numerous notes and fragments among her poems, many having their special poetical or psychological interest, are to be regarded as notes and fragments. Doubtless during the eighteen-hundred-and-nineties the very discords in her work were refreshing, and the very fragmentariness of many verses exercised a slightly provocative charm.

(Here we are, back to the attraction which the unfinished holds for us.) Mr. Lewisohn continues:

Those days are over. It is time to see clear. Here is a typical stanza:

> To lose one's faith—surpass—
> The loss of an estate
> Because estates can be
> Replenished—faith cannot.

Here the lyrical impulse, characteristic in both imaginative color and expression, failed completely after the second line. Perhaps . . . a headache came or a chain of inner association took an untoward direction. At all events, [she] added a note as to how the poem should proceed: "Because estates can be replenished, faith cannot." But the poem had not, in fact, proceeded. It had stopped dead; it is a mere cultivation of singularity to pretend otherwise. . . . She is so wealthy a poet that she has no need of her failures and fragments except for the student of her work and character. These were unique not in kind but in degree. The creative temper at its truest is always the temper that can make a great deal out of very little. . . . Thus Emily Dickinson runs true to the form of the higher creative spirits whose power is measured by intensity and not by multiplicity of experience.

Her counselor and first editor, Thomas Higginson, has been attacked for his advice against publishing her poems. Yet it would be hard to blame him if his decision had been based on certain of the manuscripts. What would any contemporary reader have made of the following, written about 1864:

> Banish Air from Air
> Divide light if you dare
> They'll meet
> While Cubes in a Drop
> Or pellets of Shape
> Fit.
> Films cannot annul
> Odors return whole
> Force Flame
> And with a Blonde push
> Over your impotence
> Flits steam.

Items of this sort are not to be confused with those poems which are intentionally rugged, even awkward, and one cannot suppose that they would have remained as they are if Emily Dickinson herself had prepared them for publication. She was most certainly capable of it, though she said: "I hesitate which word to take, as I can take but few, and each must be the chiefest; but recall that Earth's most graphic transaction is placed within a syllable, nay, even a gaze." Lacking the pressure which the finality of print exerts on most authors, she found it easier to forbear the grueling work such revision would have entailed. Our loss is small, however, in comparison to the riches that she has left to us.

Re-writing of another sort afflicts the author who deals with such an enormous mass of material as Boswell accumulated for the *Life of Johnson*. That sprawling hand has become familiar to all of us in recent years by reproductions in the daily press which accompany those stories telling of yet another truckload of papers having been found and immediately shipped to New Haven. The stories have described in detail the quantity and kind of manuscript discovered; but only when we are able to examine such chunks of it as are shown here can we form any idea of Boswell's complicated task. Journals, notes, letters, memoranda, recollections were eventually all combined into one harmonious book which remains the greatest biography of all; but no one, I think, has ever done justice to the printer. Considering the form in which the manuscript was sent to him, he might even be accorded the rank of collaborator. At all events, gentlemen, in future let us grant to Henry Baldwin, printer, the recognition he has so richly merited.

That rather terrifying *collage* which consists of some of Carlyle's research work for **Frederick the Great** makes one realize that few things survive so well as paper. Nor is it surprising to recall that Carlyle could not compress the final result into less than thirteen volumes. It is a staggering example of dogged industry, putting aside its scholarship and power of synthesis; and though I cannot claim any of those qualities, the exhibit has a vague familiarity for me: I cannot help feeling that the top of Carlyle's desk must frequently have resembled that of my own. All of us know the story that Carlyle sent the manuscript of his *French Revolution* to John Stuart Mill for annotation, and that Mill's servant unfortunately used it to light the fire. If we could believe that he had sent it in this condition, much would be explained: Mill's reluctance to annotate, and the unhappy servant's only too natural thought that this mess of stuff was intended for the fireplace. Tempting as the fantasy is, we cannot suppose that Carlyle would have sent it in such a form; besides, the whole house would have gone up in flames.

The Sinclair Lewis group has a certain morbid fascination also. Here is a novelist, not a biographer or historian, assembling a vast pile of research material, most of which he has *invented*; and this for a story of contemporary life! The distinguished critic E. M. Forster once called him a "quick spontaneous writer"—but Mr. Forster did not know his method of work. It is true that that is the impression given by his books: a long series of candid camera shots, photographic realism, those are the phrases used to describe them. It is well to bear in mind at this point that not everyone can manage a camera, too. But the way he worked was the way of the researcher, heaping up documents, real and imaginary alike, and causing his story to grow out of them. You will have observed that Babbitt's family can be traced back for three generations, and that characters from Gopher Prairie are acquainted with those from Zenith. Moreover, in these *Babbitt* worksheets there are references to *Arrowsmith*, not written until three years later. The panorama of the Middle West which Lewis depicted was a complicated and interlocking one.

W. S. Gilbert, who is represented by the manuscript of *Iolanthe*, is an example of an author whose ideas increased like amoebas. The manuscript can be opened to but one place at a time, and there was no way to show that it includes South Sea scenes which later became part of *Utopia, Ltd.*, and bits of business incorporated in *The Grand Duke*. Gilbert has been accused of repeating himself, but the manuscript can testify that many situations were worked out in a number of ways before the final one was settled on. A decisive point was reached when Gilbert wrote firmly across one page "They must be peers!" He remembered that his words were to be spoken or sung rather than read, and Sir Henry Lytton, member of the D'Oyly Carte company for many years, gives a revealing instance of this in his memoirs. In his anxiety to deliver properly the address of Robin Oakapple to the portraits of his ancestors, Lytton recited it too rapidly in the *Ruddigore* rehearsal. Gilbert, who liked to hear his own words, stopped him and began an address of his own:

> Let me tell you something. . . . That speech, "Oh my forefathers!", is now a short speech, but originally it consisted of three pages of closely-written manuscript. I condensed and I condensed. Every word I could I removed until it was of the length you find it today. Each word that is left serves some purpose—there is not one word too many. So when you know that it took me three months to perfect that one speech, I am sure you will not hurry it.

It would be possible to continue this much longer, letting the gems sift through our fingers, but we have yet to consider our main theme: the creative spirit at work. I am not one of those who hold that an esthetic achievement is merely the product of a violently diseased personality; that would seem only a variant of the Puritan theory that any lazy rogue will take to some artistic pursuit as an excuse for loafing. Whatever else these authors may have left undone, they labored intensely and long. Even the Sweet Singer of Michigan once complained that "Literary is a work very difficult to do." But work alone will not produce this kind of result. And although the personality may not be diseased, yet neither is it composed and untroubled. A. E. Housman remarks, somewhat sardonically,

> I think that the production of poetry, in its first stage, is less an active than a passive and involuntary process; and if I were obliged not to define poetry, but to name the class of things to which it belongs, I should call it a secretion; whether a natural secretion, like turpentine in a fir, or a morbid secretion, like the pearl in the oyster. I think that my own case, though I may not deal with the material so cleverly as the oyster, is the latter; because I have seldom written poetry unless I was rather out of health, and the

experience, though pleasurable, was generally agitating and exhausting.

There is an overwhelming weight of evidence that authors feel inspiration as an outside force. Plato said: "No man when in his wits, attains prophetic truth and inspiration; but when he receives the inspired word . . . he is demented by some distemper or possession." Burns said: "I have two or three times in my life composed from the wish rather than the impulse, but I never succeeded to any purpose." Stevenson said: "The real work is done by some unseen collaborator."

Of course our authors, in spite of their demoniacal possession, wrote for money, primarily. There is nothing wrong in this: the laborer is worthy of his hire. It may be somewhat disconcerting to observe Dickens in a rage because the profits from *A Christmas Carol* were so small, but possibly that merely reflected his recent close association with Scrooge. But Dickens could have earned his living in other ways; certainly he was an actor *manqué*—the immense popularity of his readings and amateur theatricals proves that. Why, then, did he write?—why did any of them write? Trollope was a successful civil servant, but wrote as industriously as though his bread and butter depended on it, instead of merely the jam. George Eliot felt that a high moral purpose was the only justification for writing fiction. Shelley and Byron were aristocrats, with no need whatever to get mixed up in this kind of thing. Ouida passionately desired celebrity—or, as it turned out, notoriety. Balzac's real ambition was to be received on equal social terms by the nobility. Emily Dickinson, as we have seen, easily abandoned the idea of publication altogether—but kept on writing. They all kept on writing.

Now very few of us, normal intelligent human beings that we are, feel impelled to sit down and turn out a long novel or an epic poem. Occasionally, since we are so intelligent, we may produce an article, the scholars among us producing a real book; but almost invariably these are factual pieces of information, designed to instruct and edify. We are not subject to frivolous impulses that force us to twist words into elaborate patterns, to polish incessantly, to sweat out rhymes, to write our work three times over, then tear it up and start it once more from the beginning.

No, this compulsion that they felt cannot be explained in any terms we understand. The nature of genius remains incomprehensible, as does its ability to transmute ordinary material into a fabric so rich as to excite awe and wonder. It was because of the need of minds like these to communicate that scribes were kept busy multiplying manuscripts, that the printing press was invented, that books became desirable possessions the world over, and that great libraries are now the pride of the nations which they serve. The glories of literature are among the few consummate achievements of mankind; and, although no one can be told how to write a great book, here before us is the way that some of them were written.

The Singular Anomalies

The exigencies of rhyme have occasionally forced even so brilliant a juggler of words as Sir William Gilbert into saying things capable of improvement. The gibe at "that singular anomaly, the lady novelist" has always seemed the poorest in Ko-Ko's celebrated catalogue; and Gilbert himself tacitly admitted as much by replacing it with half-a-dozen successive substitutions during the triumphant progress of *The Mikado* down the years. But if we begin to examine the extraordinary careers of the Victorian lady novelists, we shall observe that they may easily be regarded as anomalous and singular.

Mrs. Gore, for instance, whose fecundity was remarkable: in the course of her long career she produced some two hundred volumes, grouped mostly in clusters of three-volume novels, and ten children. Her chief literary theme was fashionable society, and she was a leading exemplar of what came to be known as the Silver Fork School. Though largely forgotten, she was at one time a rival of Thackeray; her novels treat of the same people at very nearly the same time.

Mrs. Trollope, the mother of Anthony, has nearly as impressive a record. She did not take to writing until her family's finances disintegrated, so that she was fifty-two when her first book was issued. When she published her last, she was seventy-six, and in those intervening years she had written thirty-nine other works, again mostly three-deckers. She offered a wider variety of material than Mrs. Gore: several of her novels have American settings, and some deal with industrial abuses. It is perhaps of interest to note how far we have

Based on an article written for The Princeton University Library Chronicle *(Winter, 1956), this address was read at the opening of a Grolier Club exhibition entitled* Victorian Lady Novelists *on November 18, 1969.*

progressed in that line since 1840, when her *Michael Armstrong, the Factory Boy*, was published. In that book a benevolent but impractical clergyman feels that if only some regulation could be made whereby factory children were required to work only ten hours a day, six days a week, a millennium would be achieved.

Of the more famous Brontë sisters it is scarcely necessary to speak: a torrent of books about them—critical, biographical, mythical—continues to flow till we feel that no other brief lives were ever so studied and sifted. We are more fascinated by those strange smoldering personalities and their works than were their contemporaries; but no one, then or now, ever thought of the Brontës as typical parsonage daughters.

George Eliot, that respectable flouter of convention, is even more paradoxical. Intensely earnest, preoccupied with lofty moral issues, she firmly proceeded to act in what her generation considered a most immoral manner. ("I wish," wailed Mrs. Gaskell, "oh *how* I wish Miss Evans had never seen Mr. Lewes." We may safely assume that Mrs. Gaskell had not heard of Miss Evans' residence in the fantastic household of John Chapman.)

At the Princeton University Library is a small notebook labelled simply "Quarry," which consists of notes for an unwritten novel of the Napoleonic era. As Sir Max Beerbohm said, "There is a peculiar charm for all of us in that which was still in the making when its maker died, or in that which he laid aside because he was tired of it, or didn't see his way to the end of it, or wanted to go on to something else." And that charm is very strong for us in this particular item now, because George Eliot was considering a novel with this protagonist: "Cyril Ambrose, a man of inventive power in science as well as philosophy, married young, is very poor, has a family to support, his chief ambition, the most fervid yearning of his life, is to complete the development of a philosophic system which will make an epoch in the advancing thought of mankind. But in order to maintain his family he must do work

Cyril Ambrose a man of inventive power in science as well as philosophy, married young, is very poor, has a family to support. His chief ambition, the most fervid yearning of his life, is to complete the development of a philosophic system which will make an epoch in the advancing thought of mankind. But in order to maintain his family he must do work which will bring immediate pay. He writes for newspapers, just to earn bread while he is making efforts to prevail on government to buy one of his inventions — namely, a destructive machine which will give an enormous military advantage to the power that first uses it. If he could gain a considerable sum for the invention his mind & time would be set at large. But after he has wasted much time & hope, there is no result from his applications to the English government, & he is embittered, feeling that the years are going on, & the researches necessary to give a firm basis to his system are not being made.

A page from George Eliot's *Quarry*.

which will bring immediate pay. He writes for newspapers, just to earn bread while he is making efforts to prevail on government to buy one of his inventions—namely, a destructive machine which will give an enormous military advantage to the power that first uses it."

Had George Eliot heard of Admiral Cochrane's "secret war plan"? Its nature was never made public during the 19th century though it was proposed as early as 1811 and as late as 1854—but on every occasion it was discarded as too terrible and inhuman, always with the clear admission that it was infallibly capable of destroying any fleet or fortress in the world. It needed a hundred years more of civilization before a government decided that such a plan was not too inhumane after all: in 1915 the German army used poison gas—which was Admiral Cochrane's scheme.

And now that our century has outstripped that horror with a more dreadful one, who is to re-define inhumane? We tend to think that most of the moral dilemmas which concerned the Victorians vanished with them; but unhappily this is far wide of the truth.

Mrs. Gaskell, whose exemplary life offers no such aberration as George Eliot's, nonetheless presents something of a contradiction. Best-known today as the author of *Cranford*, she is ultimately responsible for the gentle and cultivated quaintness of village tea-shoppes and all the clutter of objects associated with them; yet in her own time she was famous as the author of *Mary Barton* and *Ruth*, a hard-hitting attacker of social injustice.

Mrs. Craik managed briefly to achieve front rank among women writers, though she lacked suitable education, experience, and talent. Before she was twenty, she left her father's impecunious home and went to London. It is not easy to convey to a present day audience how staggeringly defiant of all the rules this gesture was in the eighteen-forties, but her determination carried her through. Her first novel, *The Ogilvies*, appeared in 1849, and contained a child's deathbed scene which was favorably compared to that in *Dombey and Son*, published in the previous year. Not every writer begins by rivalling Dickens!

Mrs. Craik never allowed her tremendous success in 1856 to be forgotten: every subsequent book of hers, issued by whatever publisher, bore, not merely on its title page, but on the spine, the words "*By the Author of John Halifax, Gentleman.*" She replied once to a suggestion that she change her publishers again: "As much as I can write (which is very little comparatively—on account of health and a morbid terror of 'writing myself out') but as much as I *can* write always goes to Hurst & Blackett. . . ." She need not have worried: about one hundred and thirty volumes stand to her credit, including some written for children. Incidentally, it might surprise some of those who agree with one critic that *John Halifax* is "altogether harmless, and faultlessly proper, and irredeemably commonplace," if they recalled that in their childhood they had eagerly read *The Adventures of a Brownie* and *The Little Lame Prince*.

Mary Elizabeth Braddon is not merely anomalous, she is a considerable mystery. She was born of a good family, was apparently destined for the sheltered life of a girl in the upper middle class—and then something happened—nobody knows what. She had written for amusement as a girl, Michael Sadleir tells us in *Things Past*, and a local printer offered her ten pounds for a story in 1856. Soon after this she seems to have left home, and "as early as 1860 she was supporting herself by the desperate scribbling of hack-fiction and, for a while at least, was on the stage under the name of 'Seaton.'" Should we not perhaps revise our ideas of the helpless Victorian maiden? Mr. Sadleir continues: "*Lady Audley* was published in three volumes in 1862, and almost immediately one of those mysterious and hysterical successes which now and again convulse the world of novel-publishing, caught up the book, its author and its author's future, and swept them into notoriety, and (eventually) into prosperity. From that day to this, in one form or another, *Lady Audley's Secret* has continued to sell. For forty years at least it so dominated its author's life that she had persistently to write to its pattern . . . Only in very old age was she free from the tyranny of her own fantastic popularity; . . . among her last books are two at least . . . which have not only freshness and originality, but also a quality quite different from the long series of their sensational predecessors."

Louise de la Ramée, better known as Ouida, is the most exotic figure in the company. She loved the gorgeous and the stupendous, as her novels frankly proclaim. Their settings range the world over, and their incredibly cosmopolitan heroes endeared her to a wide public: many of her forty-five novels were dramatized, and translated into several foreign languages. She is said to have invited officers of the Guards to dinner and persuaded them to talk as though she were not there, so that she might listen and later reproduce their conversation. If true, this was not the type of hospitality that most Victorian hostesses dispensed!

Marie Corelli fought against enormous disadvantages. She was illegitimate, to begin with. "She was ashamed of her mother," Virginia Woolf tells us, "She was ashamed of her birth. She was ashamed of her face, her accent, her poverty." . . . But, " 'I'll be "somebody" ' she told her governess, 'I'll be as unlike everybody else as I can!' . . . To attain that object she had only one weapon—the dream . . . She dreamt so hard, she dreamt so efficiently that with two exceptions all her dreams came true. Not even Marie Corelli could dream her shifty half-brother into the greatest of English poets . . . or transform her very dubious father into an eminent Victorian man of letters . . . Otherwise all her dreams materialized. Ponies, motor-cars, dresses, houses, gondolas, expensively bound editions of Shakespeare;—all were hers, in return for those stout volumes for which the public paid her ten thousand pounds apiece.

"Cheques accumulated. Invitations showered. The Prince

of Wales held her hand in his. Gladstone called on her and stayed two hours. On Easter Sunday the Dean of Westminster quoted her *Barabbas* from the pulpit . . . The whole audience at Stratford-on-Avon rose to its feet when she entered the theater."

She was her own press-agent: "On May Day she drove through the streets behind ponies wreathed in flowers; she floated down the Avon in a gondola called *The Dream* with a real gondolier in a scarlet sash. The press resounded with her lawsuits, her angry letters, her speeches."

Her over-riding egotism caused her not only to quarrel violently with reviewers, but to carry on the battle in her novels. One of them, *The Sorrows of Satan*, devotes a surprising amount of space to denouncing them as venal cads and ignorant brutes. Not merely that, but she installs herself as a principal figure in the story, named Mavis Clare, who comes in for a good deal of adulation from the other characters. Thus: "She . . . drives in the park in her Victoria and pair with the best in the land, and knows all the swagger people . . . I hear she's a splendid business woman and more than a match for the publishers all round . . . She is quite lovely, and knows how to dress besides . . . Most people of culture are accustomed to look upon Miss Clare as quite an exception to the usual run of authors. She is charming in herself as well as her books, and she goes everywhere. She writes with inspiration,—and always has something new to say."

As Samuel Butler remarked, the advantage of praising oneself is that one can lay it on so thick, and in exactly the right places.

This list is already long, but would be incomplete without the names of two more ladies whose popularity was great in their time.

Mrs. Henry Wood, whose *East Lynne*, published in 1881 was one of the most remarkable literary successes of the century, retained her popularity longer than most novelists. As late as 1911 a Parliamentary report stated her fiction was that most in demand among the inmates of His Majesty's prisons. And Charlotte M. Yonge scored as great a success with *The Heir of Redclyffe*, but her works appealed to those with High Church, rather than criminal, tendencies.

But what of the ladies' literary achievement? Does their work differ from that of their male counterparts? Are we inclined to offer too much praise merely to industry and determination? We must recall briefly the position of women in the early part of Victoria's reign. Those in the upper-middle class (it is chiefly from this group that our lady novelists came) had some leisure, some education. But they were barred by convention from any experience outside their home. No woman could write of war as Tolstoy did; of the London poor as Dickens did, who for years roamed the city day and night; no woman could write of the sea as Conrad was to do. Everything that women wrote of law or politics or business was at second-hand: no professions were open to them. For their books they had only two sources to rely on: their drawing-rooms and their imaginations, and out of these they did remarkably well. Not that their works are equally good, by any means, but an astonishing number of them appear to have written the Great English Novel. My own candidate for that exalted position is *Wuthering Heights*; and I have heard George Eliot's *Middlemarch* awarded the same distinction. George Moore gave this palm to—of all things—Anne Brontë's *Agnes Grey*; "The best prose fiction in English letters," he called it. In 1853 a group of Oxonians said that the best novel in the language was *The Heir of Redclyffe*. Doubtless there may have been other choices; my point is merely that despite the disadvantages women suffered from, no one dismissed these books lightly because they were written by women. For an observant woman could make good capital out of the behavior of her varied acquaintance and could train her mind to analyze character. If she moved in fashionable society, like Mrs. Gore, she had a subject ready to her hand. (Quite a number of the ladies heaped scorn on what Mr. Silas Wegg called "the minions of fashion and the worms of the hour.") If she lived in a manufacturing town, like Mrs. Gaskell, she could write of the miseries which the Industrial Revolution had created and of which Mrs. Gaskell, as a clergyman's wife, had first-hand knowledge. Familiarity with foreign countries would provide a variety of background and characters. But when all is said, these are but feeble props. Imagination—with one other element—is the important thing.

In 1897 Shaw reviewed a dramatization of *The Sorrows of Satan*, and said "Great works of fiction are the arduous victories of great minds over great imaginations." (Being Shaw, he added that "Miss Corelli's works are the cheap victories of a profuse imagination over an apparently commonplace and carelessly cultivated mind.") His definition is, I think, a good one: the quality of the author's mind does ultimately determine the quality of the fiction. Now the best minds of these Victorian ladies belonged to George Eliot and the Brontës, and it is always evident that the intellect is in control of their work.

The chief difference that strikes the reader between the ladies' books and those of male novelists is that the ladies do not sentimentalize their heroines; instead they tend to have difficulties with their heroes. George Eliot could not produce a juvenile lead fit for Maggie Tulliver; Jane Eyre's Mr. Rochester comes out of the inkstand rather than experience, and so on. But the female characters are different: they have more spirit, they are more vivid, they tend to act instead of remaining passive.

Consider, for example, the theme dear to many Victorian writers: The Fallen Woman. Let Dickens describe Martha, in *David Copperfield*:

> " 'It's a poor woman, Mas'r Davy' said Ham, 'as is trod underfoot by all the town... the mould of the churchyard don't hold any that the folk shrink away from more.... Not that I knowed then she was there, sir, but along of her creeping ... under Emily's little window, when she see the

light come, and whispering "Em'ly, Em'ly, for Christ's sake have a woman's heart towards me. I was once like you!" Those was solemn words, Mas'r Davy, fur to hear!' . . . Em'ly spoke first, 'Martha wants,' she said to Ham, 'to go to London.'

'Why to London?' returned Ham.

'Better there than here,' said a third voice aloud—Martha's, though she did not move. 'No one knows me there. Everybody knows me here.'

'She will try to do well,' said little Em'ly . . .

'I'll try,' said Martha. I can never do worse than I have done here. I may do better. Oh!' with a dreadful shiver, 'take me out of these streets, where the whole town knows me from a child!' . . . Then Martha arose, and gathering her shawl about her, covering her face with it, and weeping aloud, went slowly to the door. She stopped a moment before going out, as if she would have uttered something or turned back; but no word passed her lips. Making the same low dreary wretched moaning in her shawl, she went away."

Now Dickens had observed many such destitute women when he supervised the shelter for them that Miss Burdett-Coutts provided. He had observed many more during his London peregrinations. Yet here he produces a conventional picture, as though he were conscious that the great bulk of his audience would not tolerate the intrusion of such a creature unless she were shown to be thoroughly miserable. Martha, indeed, tends to irritate the present-day reader, to make him feel that she must change her attitude if she is to succeed in her chosen line of work, or any other.

Now listen to Ouida, who had had none of Dickens' experience. Here, from *Under Two Flags*, is the description of a kept woman, called simply the Zu-Zu:

"She was very pretty—sweetly pretty—with the clearest, sauciest eyes, and the handsomest mouth in the world; but of grammar she had not a notion, of her aspirates she had never a recollection, of conversation she had not an idea, of slang she had, to be sure, a repertoire, but to this was her command of language limited. She dressed perfectly, but she was a vulgar little soul; drank everything, from Bass's ale to rum-punch, and from cherry-brandy to absinthe ... was thoroughly avaricious, thoroughly insatiate, thoroughly heartless, pillaged with both hands, and then never had enough; had a coarse good-nature when it cost her nothing. ... The Zu-Zu was perfectly happy; and as for the pathetic picture that novelists and moralists draw, of vice sighing amid turtle and truffles for childish innocence in the cottage at home where honeysuckle bloomed and brown brooks made melody, and passionately grieving on the purple cushions of a barouche for the time of straw pallets and untroubled sleep, why—the Zu-Zu would have vaulted herself on the box seat of a drag, and told you 'To stow all that trash!' Her childish recollections were of a stifling lean-to with the odour of pigsty and strawyards, pork for a feast once a week, starvation all the other six days, kicks, slaps, wrangling, and a general atmosphere of beer and wash-tubs; she hated the past, and loved her cigar on the drag. The Zu-Zu is fact; the moralists' pictures are moonshine."

In spite of the feverish style, the frankness is welcome and carries conviction; it also explains why Ouida's books were forbidden in many households. I can think of no mid-Victorian male novelist who would have included that paragraph in his work.

Let us for a moment recall *Enoch Arden*. Tennyson's poem made so much stir that it gave rise to laws in various countries for dealing with the situation of a supposedly dead man returning home to find that his wife has remarried. Tennyson did not permit his hero to have a confrontation scene: Enoch sees that his wife is happy, and creeps silently away.

But Miss Braddon's *Lady Audley*, published a couple of years earlier, treated the matter very differently. The returning husband meets his wife, who has now married a wealthy nobleman, and who has no intention of giving up her splendid position. I cannot imagine how little Dorrit or Amelia Sedley would behave in this situation; but it may safely be said that they would not adopt Lady Audley's solution. She pushes her unwanted husband down a disused well.

I adduce this episode not to demonstrate that Miss Braddon had an especially incisive knowledge of the female of the species, but because I cannot recall a single instance even in melodramatic works by male Victorian novelists of a principal female character resorting to physical violence. Moreover, the readers of the book were not, apparently, disturbed by it, as its astounding popularity attests.

There are many respectable names I have not mentioned: Mrs. Oliphant, Mrs. Humphrey Ward, Sarah Grand, Rhoda Broughton. But I want rather to emphasize the fact that besides all these, there was a vast number of sub-literary writers who produced novels of such minimal interest that they long ago disappeared beneath the waves of oblivion. As in any period, the bulk of what was written is now forgotten; and there is no need to explore beneath the surface for such books: they were flat, insipid, characterless. One of these novelists, however, is periodically dredged up for inspection. Her two novels are so bad that they continue to fascinate numbers of people. Amanda Ros, who published *Irene Iddesleigh* in 1897, was the most highfalutin of all our authors; she was largely innocent of grammar and syntax, she cared nothing for the meaning of words, but she loved bejewelled prose. The plot of the novel is simple. Irene Iddesleigh, a penniless girl, loves her tutor, Oscar Otwell, who also has no money. She is persuaded to marry the rich Sir John Dunfern, and in due course bears him a son. But she continues to love Oscar, and one day Sir John discovers this. He instantly confines her to an upper room where, he tells her, she must pass the rest of her life. She escapes, of course, and joins her Oscar, but, alas, they have no money. They sell a house that doesn't belong to them, and with the proceeds flee across the Atlantic to Dobbs Ferry, here on the Hudson. Oscar has a job teaching, and for a time all goes well, but eventually they discover that they have no money. Oscar takes to drink and drowns himself, and Irene makes her way back to England to beg forgiveness of Sir John. I will quote the passage which describes her arrival at the Dunfern mansion:

> "Gently ringing the bell, the door was attended by a strange face. Reverently asking to have an interview with Sir John Dunfern, how the death-like glare fell over the eyes of the disappointed as the footman informed her of his demise! 'Madam, if you cast your eyes thence—[here the sturdy footman pointed to the family graveyard, lying quite adjacent, and in which the offcast of effrontery had oftentimes trodden]—you can with ease behold the rising symbol of death which the young nobleman, Sir Hugh Dunfern, has lavishly and unscrupulously erected to his fond memory.'"

Irene then wanders off and dies that night.

This nightmare of nonsense may be taken to represent the nadir of the works we have been discussing; and it is a far, far cry from the magnificent achievement which the best of the books are. Merely summoning up the titles of the innumerable three-deckers, one seems to hear the faint, constant scratching of many pens. What energy they had! They wrote endlessly. They wrote masterpieces and twaddle. They wrote sermons and poems and polemics and tracts, all in the guise of fiction. They wrote for every possible reason: Ouida craved celebrity, Mrs. Craik had her 'vocation,' Marie Corelli sought a new identity for herself, George Eliot held that the paramount purpose in writing was to teach. Above all, they wrote for money: Mrs. Trollope had a family to support, Miss Yonge helped outfit a missionary schooner, Mrs. Oliphant undertook to pay for the education of her brother's children as well as that of her own, Miss Braddon spent years extricating her future husband from a crushing debt. They wrote as a task, a habit, a passion.

On the whole, they may well be called singular anomalies: Ko-Ko was right. Certainly they deviated from the common rule. But his conclusion was wrong—they would have been missed, they would be missed, very much indeed.

Max Beerbohm's Literary Credo

Max Beerbohm was born in 1872. Anyone discussing him must cling to a few such indisputable facts because he is surrounded by so many inexplicable paradoxes. Max was a quiet, introspective man; but he was engaged to two actresses before marrying a third. He was a sought-after guest at Edwardian house-parties, admired for his wit, his elegance, his pleasing personality; but when he married, he abruptly left this milieu, and exiled himself and his wife to a tiny villa at Rapallo. Two world wars dislodged him and sent him back to England; but after each was over he returned to Italy. He loved that country; but in forty years' residence there, he never learned Italian.

He developed a brilliant literary style, but many of his manuscripts testify that he would rather sketch than write. Yet his drawings—or rather, caricatures: they are always of people—almost invariably require the often lengthy captions which he supplied.

And his character repeated these unexpected combinations. He was, as Lord David Cecil says, "civilized yet simple, modest yet self-confident, pessimistic yet cheerful, sensitive yet somehow invulnerable."

He began his professional career in the nursery. The exhibition starts with an album containing drawings made before he was ten; and he displayed little more skill then than did the rest of us at that age. But there is one difference: the drawings are all of people: no animals, no houses, no landscape. Almost from the beginning he was fascinated by celebrities, and, oddly for a child, by politicians and statesmen in particular. As a youngster, he loitered outside 10 Downing Street

An address delivered at the opening of the Grolier Club exhibition entitled The Works of Max Beerbohm *on 21 December 1971.*

to watch the well-known figures come and go. Thus early did a lasting interest display itself.

He continued drawing at his school, Charterhouse, contributing to the school magazine; and Charterhouse also saw his first literary publication. He wrote a set of Latin elegiacs, called *Carmen Becceriense*, making fun of the recitals given by the music master, and added pseudo-scholarly notes which occasionally referred disparagingly to his Latin teacher. Here in this first attempt at parody we find one of his mature characteristics: Max enjoyed making fun of people more if he respected or was supposed to respect them. In general, he liked things better if he could laugh at them.

He went to Oxford in 1890, where he thoroughly enjoyed himself. It was not merely the adult freedom after school discipline (he said once that "undergraduates owe their happiness chiefly to the consciousness that they are no longer at school. The nonsense that was knocked out of them at school is all put gently back at Oxford.") But in addition there was the intellectual atmosphere—not too oppressive, for Beerbohm had no philosophic bent—and the aestheticism of the period: Walter Pater was still lecturing, and undergraduates still debated the best ways of experiencing "delicate joys" and "exquisite sorrows" and of "burning with a hard, gem-like flame." (Max, incidentally, says that he read *Marius the Epicurean* at school, regarding it "as a tale of adventure, quite as fascinating as *Midshipman Easy*, and far less hard to understand, because there were no nautical terms in it.") Moreover, Oxford, though tending to look down on London, kept open the connections to that great world outside. All of this pleased Beerbohm, who made many friends while continuing to meditate and draw caricatures.

In 1892 *The Strand Magazine* published a series of his drawings called *Club Types*, his first professional publication. In 1893 his half brother, the actor-manager Beerbohm Tree, produced Oscar Wilde's *A Woman of No Importance*, and Max met Wilde and Lord Alfred Douglas. In 1894 *The Yellow Book* made its appearance. It is difficult now to understand the storm of disapproval aroused by that rather pallid publication. "A combination of English rowdiness and French lubricity," said the *Times*, while *The Westminster Gazette* called for "an act of Parliament to make this kind of thing illegal." Max had been asked by Aubrey Beardsley to contribute to the volume, and his *Defence of Cosmetics* was one of the items savagely attacked by the reviewers. The fact that some of the articles, including Beerbohm's, were not meant to be taken seriously did not occur to these critics.

In 1895 Beerbohm Tree and his company crossed the Atlantic for an American tour, and he took his young half-brother along as private secretary. Max, who had left Oxford without taking a degree, enjoyed the trip very much. Beerbohm Tree soon found it necessary to engage another secretary, for Max spent so much time on the style of his answers that he got hopelessly behindhand. Released from secretarial duties, he wrote several essays which were bought by *Vanity Fair* and *The Chapbook*, and he made and sold several drawings. In that brief six-weeks' visit he became well enough known to be asked if he would give a series of lectures. This, indeed, he declined—not for half a century was he to do anything of that sort—but the offer indicates that the youth of twenty-three had become a personality. Moreover, on this tour he fell in love with and proposed to the first of his three actresses.

He returned to England and made new friends—John Davidson, Charles Conder, and other figures associated with the nineties. And he continued drawing caricatures, which he always found easier than writing. In 1896 appeared his first collection in book form—*Caricatures of Twenty-five Gentlemen*. And *The Happy Hypocrite*, which had appeared in Vol. IX of *The Yellow Book*, proved so popular that John Lane issued it separately in wrappers—Max's first fantasy in book form. In addition, Lane brought out a collection of essays Max had published in various periodicals. This, in a neat red cloth binding, was grandiosely called *The Works of Max Beerbohm*, and Lane even furnished a bibliography for it.

These publications, slight as they were, established him. He was no longer a coming writer; at the age of twenty-four he had arrived. Edmund Gosse invited him to an afternoon gathering, and in 1896 this meant a great deal to a young writer: it was a literary accolade that had to be earned. Max later said: "My *Works* had just been published and to Gosse, whom I had met often enough, I sent a copy. He was not quick to patronize young men who had done nothing, nor those who had done nothing good.... I remember that when I received my summons to Delamere Terrace I felt that my little book really had not fallen flat. The drawing room was very full when, carefully dressed for the part of a brilliant young dandy, and very calm, and very shy, I made my entry." It was through Gosse that he met other important people in the world of arts and letters—such people as Whistler and Henry James.

That year also there was a further significant publication. The Christmas supplement of the *Saturday Review* contained parodies of six writers: George Meredith, H. G. Wells, Richard LeGallienne, Alice Meynell, Marie Corelli, and Beerbohm himself. Each was represented as writing on some aspect of Christmas and the whole was entitled *A Christmas Garland*. It was to develop into Max's masterpiece in this vein, the *Christmas Garland* of 1912.

Meanwhile, his social life was broadening to include what used to be called wealth, rank, and fashion. His name began to appear in the visitors' books of various great houses. This was a novel experience for him. The Beerbohm family had never been more than comfortable, and after Max's father had died in 1891, the household was considerably straitened. Max lived with his mother and sisters, but could contribute little to current expenses. Payment for his articles was small, and he learned early to content himself with modest expenditure. Indeed, he did that all his life, for he was never to earn much from his work. Without desiring luxury, however, it was easy to enjoy his first taste of it. But his pleasure was largely amusement, as usual. He wrote to Reginald Turner while staying with the Harmsworths in Kent: "I hope to see much of the Harmsworths—cigarettes and a telephone by one's bedside, and an enormous peach with one's morning tea, and a glass of sherry-and-bitters on one's dressingtable at night-fall, and bound volumes of Vanity Fair in the library, and two small alligators in one of the innumerable hothouses, and generally all the things which are indispensable to a scholar and a gentleman."

No, his head was not turned. He knew that this atmosphere, congenial though it was at times, could not be his home. And in any case there was the problem of earning money. Unexpectedly, in the spring of 1898, came the offer of a job. Bernard Shaw, dramatic critic of the *Saturday Review*, decided to resign and recommended Beerbohm as his successor. The editor, Frank Harris, agreed, and Max was persuaded to undertake the only regular employment of his life. He found it difficult. Though he had known the theater all his life, it was not the form of art he most enjoyed; and turning out a weekly essay was, for this fastidious craftsman, a considerable effort. But he comforted himself with the thought that it would not last long; and meanwhile it paid him five badly needed pounds a week. It lasted twelve years.

Again he had received unusual recognition: for a youth of twenty-six to be offered this post on an important weekly was astonishing; and his merit secured him the offer, for he was not on really intimate terms with either Shaw or Harris, and never became so.

He had time to continue his own work, and a few months after beginning work with the *Saturday Review* he had conceived a fantasy more ambitious than anything he had previously attempted: its setting was Oxford, its theme the appearance there of a girl so fascinating that all the undergraduates were driven to drown themselves for love of her. Even her name was decided on: Zuleika Dobson. But another thirteen years would elapse before the story was finished.

I have been thus detailed about his early achievements because they indicated precisely the lines his mature work was to take. By the age of twenty-six he had adumbrated all his later career. From then on there was improvement but no innovation. Even the broadcasts that he made during World War II can be bracketed with the lectures he was asked to give in 1895.

I shall offer no criticism of his books, because I hope that what follows will prove more interesting. From three unpublished letters by Max we may learn much of his feeling about his own work and his own ideals and personal standards.

The first example was written in irritation. In spite of that, perhaps because of it, we get an unequivocal opinion of his literary position, and of the way the presentation of his work reinforces its quality.

>March 6, 1916
>*To the Editor of* The Century Magazine
>
>Dear Sir—I send in another envelope the corrected proofs of my two stories—"Enoch Soames" and "A. V. Laider." Every page of these is scored all over with corrections. But I am not to blame: I am not giving any unnecessary trouble. On the contrary, I am to be pitied for the great amount of unnecessary trouble that has been imposed on me. I have not added anything that wasn't in my M.S., nor have I subtracted anything that was there. I have readily fallen in with your wishes that I shouldn't alter the Century Dictionary spelling . . . . (Indeed, your wishes in this matter are mine. The one important thing in spelling is not to give the reader a "jump." In writing for an American magazine, one prefers the spelling that is most familiar to Americans.) Furthermore, the number of my corrections in these proofs is not due to any *carelessness* on the part of your

48, Upper Berkeley Street
London W
March 6, 1916

To the Editor of The Century Magazine

Dear Sir,
            I send the corrected proofs of my two
stories — "Enoch Soames" and "A. V. Laider." Every page of these is
scored all over with corrections. But I am not to
blame: I am not giving any unnecessary trouble. On the contrary,
I am to be pitied for the great amount of unnecessary trouble
that has been imposed on me. I have not added anything
that wasn't in my M.S.; nor have I subtracted anything that was
there. I have readily fallen in with your wish that I shouldn't
alter the Century Dictionary spelling — "envelop" (instead of "envelope"), "honor", "defense",
and so forth. (Indeed your wishes in this matter are mine. The one
important thing in spelling is not to give the reader a "jump." In
writing for an American magazine, I prefer the spelling that is most
familiar to Americans.) Furthermore, the number of my corrections in
these proofs is not due to any carelessness on the part of your printers
and proof-readers. It is due merely to their crude and asinine
interference with my punctuation, with my division of
paragraphs, and with other details ... Details? No, these are not
details to me. My choice of stops is as important to me — as important
for the purpose of conveying easily to the reader my exact shades of meaning — as my
choice of words ... Please don't think I am taking up a "high-and-mighty"
attitude. I am very well aware that I am not a great or
heaven-inspired writer. But I am equally well aware that I am
a very careful, conscientious, skilled craftsman in literature. And
it is most annoying for me to find my well-planned
effects repeatedly destroyed by the rough-and-ready, standardising
methods of your proof-readers. These methods are, no doubt, very
salutary, and necessary, in the case of gifted but illiterate or
careless contributors to your magazine. But I, personally, will
none of them. And if, at any future date, you do me the
honour to accept any other piece of my writing, please let
it be understood that my M.S. must be respected, not pulled
about and put into shape in accordance to any schoolmasterly notion
of how authors ought to write.

            Meanwhile, the corrections in these two proofs will necessitate
a good deal of rearrangement of the type. In a vast number

Draft of Beerbohm's letter to the editor of The Century Magazine.

printers and proof-readers. It is due merely to their crude and asinine interference with my punctuation, with my division of paragraphs, and with other details . . . Details? No, these are not details to me. My choice of stops is as important to me—as important for the purpose of conveying easily to the reader my exact shades of meaning—as my choice of words. Please don't think I am taking up a "high-and-mighty" attitude. I am very well aware that I am not a great or heaven-inspired writer. But I am equally well aware that I am a very careful, conscientious, skilled craftsman in literature. And it is most annoying for me to find my well-planned effects repeatedly destroyed by the rough-and-ready, *standardizing* methods of your proof-readers. These methods are, no doubt, very salutary, and necessary, in the case of gifted but illiterate or careless contributors to your magazine. But I, personally, will none of them. And if, at any future date, you do me the honour to accept any other piece of my writing, please let it be understood that my M.S. must be respected, and not pulled about and put into shape according to any school-masterly notion of how authors ought to write.

Meanwhile, the corrections in these two proofs will necessitate a good deal of rearrangement of the type. In a vast number of cases, my "strokes" were replaced by commas. These "strokes" I have religiously replaced. "Strokes" occupy far more space than do commas, and therefore, unless the lines are to be unpleasantly congested with type, there will have to be plenty of translineation. I don't know whether there is such a word as "translineation" in the Century Dictionary. (My volumes of that very admirable work are at my home in Italy, and not available for reference at this moment.) I fancy that I have just coined the word. In case its meaning is obscure, let me say that I mean the carrying down of the last word in a line into the next line, and of the last word in the next line into the next-but-one, and so on, to the end of the paragraph.

Please give instructions to the printers that all this is to be done carefully.

                I am, dear Sir
                Yours very truly,

The second letter, a reply to A.J.A. Symons, who was compiling a bibliography, has more mixed emotions. We feel that Max queried the value of such a project, and consequently his irony flickers over the whole surface, flaring into a malicious bit of teasing in the postscript.

                Italy
                March 1, 1926

Dear Mr. Symons. You do me great honour. You do me too great honour. I cannot help feeling that my existence has caused you to waste a great deal of precious time. And no doubt I shall have to answer for this waste on the Last Day —whereas the fault is entirely your own, as I shall shriekingly point out while I am being hustled away from the Bar and cast down into the Flames. And in the meantime you—you!—ask me to "help" you! Under the vast piles of masonry that you have reared over me, how can I lift a little finger? How can I even draw my last breath? I am suffocated; I have no last breath to draw. That curse on you which would be the natural accompaniment of that last breath cannot be uttered. You have nothing to fear from me.

And little to hope. Those infinite galley-proofs of yours appear to be overflowing with accuracy. Nowhere does my glazing eye perceive a mistake—except in the note on "A Peep Into the Past." I gather from a bookseller's catalogue that the publisher (whoever he may be) says, as *you* say, that the thing was written for the *Yellow Book*. But it was not so. It was just a squib to amuse a few people. Naturally I am annoyed by the piracy. Will you please alter the Note thus:—"This work is a reproduction in facsimile of an entertaining squib in which Oscar Wilde, then at the height of his celebrity, is written of as a journalist long since forgotten. It is a pirated work—published without any authorization from Mr. Beerbohm." (You use the word "entertaining" and I trust your judgement of what I very dimly remember.)

[*Max goes on to mention certain periodicals and annuals to which he has contributed. He continues:*] You have certainly mentioned all the books I have introduced. The book about my brother is the only one that I have edited. I have never translated anything—except some Latin and Greek and French, when I was at school. It is awful to think that my old exercise books are lost forever and beyond reach of your measurements.

Talking of translations, I do possess a copy of Marcel Boulestin's French rendering of "The Happy Hypocrite," which you say you haven't seen. [*Max then furnishes a laborious description occupying a quarto page, and adds:*] Isn't all this absolutely THRILLING?

How little does mankind dream of the boon it is to receive from me through you! Mankind walks in darkness—or rather, stumbles there. Patience, mankind! The dawn is at hand.

But, though I speak thus, please, dear Mr. Symons, don't let mankind know of it. I mean, please don't say in your preface that you wish to tender your warmest thanks to Mr. Beerbohm, who has rocked the cradle of this book with a solicitude almost maternal and with a brooding smile surpassed only by that of Carlo Dolci's madonnas, and that but for his hawk-like swiftness in swooping on inaccuracies, and his coal-heaver-like strength and steadiness in unloading facts hitherto unknown, you could never have, etc., etc.

I mean don't make any reference of any sort to me in your table of thanks and don't anywhere in the bibliography itself quote me as an authority. For if mankind knew I had helped you, mankind would think me a vain and fussy person, in love with homage and advertisement, and not gifted with a sense of proportion. And really and truly I am not that sort of person—am I?

With very many thanks for your charming letter, and with all best wishes, I am
Yours sincerely,
Max Beerbohm

P.S. I have only one anonymous publication to confess. Or rather, a pseudonymous one. "What Joshua Would Say For Us" by an Evangelical Imperialist. It was the third of a series of pamphlets published by the All-Britain League shortly before the Boer War. I was very hard up at the time, otherwise I would not have written it. I am now rather ashamed of it. It is crude (though bright and forceful) stuff—or seems so to me. The measurements are as follows:

. . . alas, I can't find my copy. Please therefore abstain from any mention of this work.

What a devilish thing to do to a bibliographer! And how plausibly the misinformation was spread out for him! At last the author would provide a hitherto-unrecorded item—but no, the author did nothing of the kind. Max's impishness remained with him to the end.

The reference in this letter to *A Peep Into the Past* reminds me that he dealt more at length with the problem of piracy in the preface to the American edition of *A Variety of Things*. He dealt with it, as we shall see, logically, cogently, and all but convincingly. For I do not believe that any collector was ever stimulated by this passage to surrender any piracy he may have had. Rather, alas, would he make sure that no such item had eluded him.

Here is the quotation: "I suggest that American collectors should leave unbought any book as to which they are not sure that the author sanctioned its issue. After all, the reason (I had almost said, the excuse) for desiring first editions of an author whose work one likes is that they give one a sense of nearness to him. . . . This is the binding *he* chose—perhaps. This—perhaps—is the fount of type that *he* insisted on. Here certainly is a typographical error that *his* eye overlooked—

bless his noble spirit! . . . I urge that there is nothing like piracy to give one a sense of remoteness from one's favorite . . . This is the book *he* didn't know was going to be published. These are the very pages *he* always refused to glance at. What wouldn't one give to possess, on a velvet pad under a glass case, the one single cent *he* never received for his work! Here is a marble bust of the publisher. The brow is magnificent, isn't it?"

The third-and-final letter was never finished and no version of it, so far as I know, was ever mailed. Elinor Wylie's publisher sent Max a copy of her first novel, *Jennifer Lorn.* Max was almost boundlessly delighted by the felicities of the book—and equally annoyed by careless passages and phrases. But the real reason for the length of his commentary is the fact that Miss Wylie's aim was what had often preoccupied Max himself—to produce a beautifully-written fantasy that would have the shimmer of the Comic Spirit woven into it. Let Max's enthusiasm—sustained for longer than usual with him—speak for itself.

> Dear Madam. Your publisher has been so good as to send me a copy of "Jennifer Lorn."
>
> I don't often read a book which I feel I should like to have written myself. But I should like very much to have written "Jennifer Lorn." "I should rather think you would!" you reply. To which I rejoin that tho' my powers are slight enough, my judgement is extremely good, and that my poor fond wish ought therefore to give you a little pleasure—even in the midst of the loud chorus of praise that (I hope) your book will have.
>
> I am, dear Madam
> Yours very . . . . but this letter is

too short for the long journey it is going to take. My eye wanders to the copy of "Jennifer" that lies on my table. I am very much in the habit of marking, in a book that interests me, passages that I like especially; also passages that seem to me wrong. I have marked an immense number of much-liked things in "Jennifer;" and a few small lapses—or what seem to me lapses. And it is a fine afternoon, and I've nothing to do, and authors are rather apt to want to know what other people think; and so—tho' it would be much easier and more pleasant if you yourself were here—let me go through my copy of "Jennifer" with you . . . pedantically, marked page by page.

Page 11. The proleptic touch. I believe very much in that device—I immediately became interested.

Page 26. Before I came to this I had become more than interested. "Here," I had said, "is a woman who can WRITE" [sacred word!—and sacred function in which your sex so rarely partakes to advantage] "and is a born and made ironist, and has in virtue of her irony a keen scent for the 18th century, and has fancy, and wit, *and*" added I, after reading the passage about the gardener, "great sense of beauty and tenderness and fun."

Page 29.—"utterly charming"—neither of these is a word of the period. Pray retract them from future editions. You do the language of the time so well—or rather, you suggest it so well. It's a thing a modern writer had much better *suggest* than *do*. The Zounds,—I-am-monstrous-glad, egad, style is very quickly intolerable. Just sound good lucid formal graceful English (like yours) is the right way to suggest 18th century speech. Of course in a fantastic novel the formality may be fantasticated to any extent. And this you do delightfully, with great sensitiveness to the possible absurdities latent in language. In fact, you are utterly charming. I may be allowed to say that. But you should not have allowed Mr. Poynyard to say it of the little Solange. They break the absurd antique spell that you have been weaving.

Page 96. A lovely first sentence. Also the proleptic touch again. Oh, there's so much to be said for that, in narrative art. But I won't bore you and me by saying it. Enough to say how poignant it makes pages 125–130.

Are you bored? No; I believe this is just the sort of letter an author likes to receive. I have never written one of this kind before. But it is such a fine afternoon.

Page 37. A dead man cannot be knighted nor made a baronet. Besides, you aren't the British Sovereign. Why this attempt on the memory of Mr. Horace Walpole?

Page 84. "subsequent upon the non-arrival." Oh, good heavens! What sort of wretched muddy commercial jargon is this? *You*, with your elegance and limpidity, aren't you very much ashamed? Purify, please, for future editions. There will be many future editions, I am sure. Whether or not the book is an instant success, there will always in future years be discerning enthusiasts persuading a fair number of people to read it. A fantasy so well-inspired as yours, and so tightly-wrought, will not cease to be appreciated, I am very sure.

Page 117. Another gaffe. "a good twenty years my deceased uncle's junior." Dreadful, isn't it? How Robert Louis Stevenson, whom by many tokens I judge you admire, would have squirmed in reading it! But how enthusiastic he would have been about the whole work!—the delicacy and the prettiness and the endless fun of it; and (vastly important) the good solid *construction*, whereby you keep the interest up to the last page of all.

Page 118. "an apparently wholly." Perhaps it's as well that the aforesaid Stevenson didn't live to read you and be killed by that awful collision of two adverbs. Avert such collisions.

Pages 122–3. "In all the strange and varied trials and adventures of his later years the memory of that night remained intact and perfect, like a pastoral scene upon a coach panel, or a classic instance modelled in tinted clay." —I copy out that sentence just for the pleasure of copying it out. It is a fine example of your sure sense for cadence— and of your amusingness, too. Not that these two things can be separated, strictly. Part of the beauty of the cadence is in its amusingness—in its expression and intensification of the fun.

Page 124. "Painted succeeded"—another awful collision —or smash, as I believe such things are called in your country. *Appalling Loss of Life. Death of the Ghost of R. L. Stevenson.*

Do forgive me these niggling criticisms. It is because you have such a rare notion of the architecture of sentences, and of the right ornamentation of them that these occasional slight bungles stand out to my vision and worry me and move me to worry *you* about them. Perhaps you have more sense of proportion than I, and ask "Why is this old fool wasting his time?" I can only repeat (in a cracked senile voice) that it is a most lovely afternoon, and feebly resume:

Page 127. "It was simple, since the child was tired, to add a touch of rose-colour to the counterfeited cheek, instead of demanding a rouge-box and hare's foot to improve the pallor of the true one." Those last seven words! Brava! Congratulations on your ear. *Ear:* that is one of the main requisites in a writer, don't you think? What's Brain without Ear? But these are dark and difficult speculations. Return we to Jennifer.

P. 133. "consequently extremely." *Another Horrible Catastrophe. Ghost of R.L.S. Re-Mangled.*

Pages 137–8. The paragraph about Jennifer and Diderot. One of your most exquisitely absurd and touching things. I wonder if you like it as much as I do. Probably not. The things one likes best are, naturally, the things one could'nt have done oneself.

P. 147. "In this as in other matters the thin eggshell of the future was transparent to his pale and voracious eye." How do you do it?

P. 164. Jennifer reading the "Ode to Evening:" "the assurance that it occupied no more than two printed pages encouraged her to read further." How well, oh how well I know that feeling! Thank you for expressing it so tersely. For me even the best poems—and even perhaps especially the best—but I stifle the confession. Enough that Jennifer's need of "encouragement," that glance of hers ahead, endeared her more than ever to me, and more than ever interested me in her fate. Therefore, I wonder if you share her weakness and are reassured by the sight of only "two printed pages." Talking of brevity, how about this letter? Talking about two pages, here I am on my eighth!—and yet only at the 164th of yours, which has 302, and ever so many marked ones in the remainder. . . . Lifting my eyes, I see a slight cloud on the horizon; and I falteringly murmur, "Long live Brevity!" For her sake and yours and mine I will say no more. No more details, at any rate. Merely a general congratulation or two, on this and that. On, for example,

The letter breaks off here in mid-sentence. But not before it has revealed to us more of Max's literary credo than is to be found in any other single source. The elements it touches on, again and again, are just those which characterize Max's best work. Beauty, cadence, amusingness, the absurdities latent in language, tenderness, irony, a sense of fun: these are, all of them, his characteristics. They are not, perhaps, very fashionable ones today; and at no time did they impress those who believed that the mind and spirit should be harrowed for their own good. Pity and terror are not invoked for us in Max's caricatures and writings; they offer something quieter and less exciting, but something, none the less, that was never common. Now that we are in another set of times that try men's souls, we encounter that something more rarely than ever. But Max offers it to us in words and drawings in full measure —the simple and satisfying quality of delight.

III

ANTHONY TROLLOPE

Portrait Drawing of Anthony Trollope by Samuel Lawrence (1864).

On Rereading *Barchester Towers*

Poetry, most of us would say, is the special province of the creative imagination; and yet is not prose equally illuminated by it? Certainly it flashes through the English novel in a dazzling variety of ways. The fearful and exultant universe of *Wuthering Heights*, the remote matter-of-fact world of *Robinson Crusoe*, the microcosm of comedy that shimmers in *The Egoist*—none of these is more than familiar material transmuted by a novelist's imagination.

Not always, however, do we recognize this quality; it is particularly difficult to do so in a work dealing with ordinary characters moving among everyday scenes. This unheroic theme, we tend to feel, is only the surface of life, this is mere reporting, this anyone could write, if . . . if. . . . But we are wrong. Few writers fathom the wellsprings of life, and most readers prefer less adventurous territory. After all, the surface of life is as much a part of it as the core, demanding hardly less skill to represent it fitly. Tales over which we linger and to which we return are those that convince us of their truth, whether they tell of the inner spirit or the commonplace round. And this power of conviction, displayed so genially in *Barchester Towers*, is Anthony Trollope's greatest gift.

This was the novel with which Trollope found his stride and his public. True, it was written as a continuation of *The Warden*; but the earlier book appears slightly tentative and experimental when compared with the sequel. Moreover, though *The Warden* is more concise (being one of the short-

This article was written as an introduction to Trollope's novel in the Oxford Illustrated Trollope. But when that ill-fated venture collapsed, it was used for the same work when it appeared in the World's Classics edition (1960) after having been published in the Autumn 1953 issue of The Princeton University Library Chronicle.

est novels its author ever wrote), the greater length of *Barchester Towers* gave Trollope the scope he was always to need for his best work. His method, style, and indeed his whole theory of fiction were well suited by a loose rambling plot which left the characters free to develop and disport themselves as they chose. It was by the slow accretion of an infinity of subtle touches that he achieved his effects, and the rigorous pruning which might sometimes have improved the pace of his stories would surely have destroyed their charm.

Miss Thorne's *fête champêtre*, for instance, occupies eight whole chapters of *Barchester Towers*, though it contributes little to the action; but who would wish to lose a single word of it? Our delight is in watching nearly all the county of Barset accept Miss Thorne's hospitality, and in feeling, as the throng streams into the grounds of Ullathorne, that we are borne along with it, well acquainted alike with Stubbs and the Greenacres, with the De Courcys and the bishop. Much of Trollope's superb character-drawing lies in the exquisite nicety of relationship that his people bear to each other, and this in turn is the result of his constant preoccupation with them. He devoted his spare time for two and a half years to the brief *Warden* (he tells us that in later life when he had mastered his craft it would not have cost him more than six weeks), and he spent eighteen months on *Barchester Towers*. He thoroughly knew his characters and all that was in their minds and why they acted as they did. It is easy to understand how, without question, his books have come to be considered the best representation of mid-Victorian England; and here, in this novel, is the first of the many panoramic views he gave us.

A loosely-knit narrative, however, offers frequent opportunities for digression, which we find so annoying today, and Trollope made full use of these occasions. His ability to maintain the interest of his story while taking persistent liberties is extraordinary. Though he interrupts, speaking in his own person, assuring us that Eleanor is not in love with Mr. Slope, that Bertie will not succeed in marrying her, yet the thread is never quite broken. Once or twice he so contrives these appeals that we cease to resent them, as when Mrs. Quiverful makes her way to Mrs. Proudie by tipping the footman: " 'I must see her'; and she put her card and half-crown—think of it, my reader, think of it; her last half-crown—into the man's hand. . . ." And whatever irritation these intrusions may cause, it is a trifling price for the rich satisfaction of many excellencies.

These are often unexpected: to encounter the careless Stanhopes, those unthrifty hedonists, in a sedate cathedral town is very surprising. How alive they are, and how entertaining! Note them well, for they will not appear in subsequent books, as other characters will. The publisher's reader in 1857 thought the Signora Neroni "a great blot on the work" and there was some risk of her being suppressed altogether. But she and her brother Bertie were spared, to remind us that every era produces its own Bright Young Things. Bertie, moreover, is Trollope's one successful attempt at depicting an artist. We believe entirely in the cleverness of Bertie's caricatures, although we are not in the least convinced in the later novels by Conway Dalrymple's painting, Isadore Hamel's sculpture, or Rachel O'Mahony's singing. Bertie has only a minor role in the book, but we remember him—it is not easy to forget his polite effort at small talk during the episcopal reception ("I was a Jew once myself"), or his half-hearted and too honest love-making.

Another character we shall not meet elsewhere is Obadiah Slope. Trollope hints his descent from Sterne's Dr. Slop; and the name of his more immediate ancestor has a curiously similar ring: Uriah Heep. The methods of Dickens and Trollope can be briefly illuminated by this instructive comparison. Messrs. Heep and Slope are scheming, ambitious hypocrites, each physically repulsive to the reader, each exuding oily politeness when there is anything to be got by it, and each plotting to avenge his slights and marry the heroine—but what a difference between them! Uriah Heep is all violent contrasts and impossible melodrama; yet Dickens endows him with such triumphant vitality that he sticks like a burr in our memory. The offensive Slope earns our dislike in a milder, more plausible manner. We rejoice when the signora punishes him; but since he did battle bravely with Mrs. Proudie, something may be forgiven him. Trollope himself was willing to bestow a sugar-refiner's widow on this most disagreeable of his clergymen.

Mention of the clergy brings up the scene of the novel. The genesis of *The Warden*—and consequently of the other Barsetshire tales—was Trollope's visit to Salisbury in the course of an official Post Office inspection, as is well known; but it is curious to reflect that he *invented* that authentic Church of England atmosphere, those characters that seem the product of the acutest observation. "I never lived in any cathedral city," he says in *An Autobiography*, "except London, never knew anything of any Close, and at that time had enjoyed no peculiar intimacy with any clergyman. My archdeacon, who has been said to be life-like, and for whom I confess that I have all a parent's fond affection, was, I think, the simple result of an effort of my moral consciousness . . . an archdeacon was produced who has been declared by competent authorities to be a real archdeacon down to the very ground. And yet, as far as I can remember, I had not then ever spoken to an archdeacon."

He was not familiar, we see, with clerical society, or with church problems and administration, except what he picked up from newspaper attacks on church abuses. Moral consciousness did it all. We may well feel, then, that moral consciousness is valuable equipment, especially when backed by common sense, a gift for story-telling, and an unfaltering interest in ordinary people. As Somerset Maugham has pointed out, "The ordinary is the writer's richer field. Its unexpectedness, its singularity, its infinite variety afford unending material. The great man is too often all of a piece; it is the little man that is a bundle of contradictory elements. He is inexhaustible." Trollope anticipated the wisdom of this, and succeeded despite his ignorance of the setting. For he treated his deans and vicars, his rectors and curates, as ordinary men, thereby making them wholly real to us, and avoided showing them in the exercise of their spiritual functions. From time to time one of them preaches a sermon; but what we hear of it illustrates merely the human failings of that particular preacher. We are told that Mr. Arabin, who as a young man "sat for a while at the feet of the great Newman," had meditated about going over to Rome—and this little episode is the only reference to the Oxford Movement, which in its day had set every parsonage in England buzzing and had rocked the Established Church. Trollope writes of behavior, not doctrine. Some of his ecclesiastical details are open to criticism—and have received it—but we may leave the sensitive experts to worry over such matters. It is almost possible to argue that his lack of acquaintance with such clergymen as he describes set his pen free; certainly when he did choose a background that he knew well, the result was sometimes inferior. *The Three Clerks*, which followed *Barchester Towers*, deals with the Civil Service, and Trollope, who worked half his life in the Post Office, was naturally at home in this setting. Nonetheless, we are far more willing to forgive any churchly error in the Barsetshire novels than we are to pardon the chapter on Civil Service reform that he could not bring himself to exclude from *The Three Clerks*.

In 1860 Hawthorne, praising Trollope's works, wondered whether they were known in America and added: "It needs an English residence to make them thoroughly comprehensible, but still I should think that the human nature in them would give them a success anywhere." An English residence will no longer familiarize anyone with the customs of Trollope's time; but in fact it was never necessary. This most British of novelists was greatly admired by his contemporaries in the United States, and American editions of various titles, particularly *Barchester Towers*, have since testified to his continued popularity.

This novel, by the way, is something of a touchstone: many

persons prefer other works by Trollope, but he who dislikes *Barchester Towers* will dislike them all. It contains the author's faults and virtues in profusion, and most of them are obvious to the quickest glance. But the chief characteristic, which nowadays we seize on so gratefully, is the mellow kindliness that informs each page and has made it the best known of all his tales.

It achieved that eminence slowly. The cautious publisher at first refused to pay Trollope an advance of even one hundred pounds for it (at the height of his career his books were to bring him thirty times as much), and, though the critics were, on the whole, very favorable, the sale was small. Three months after its publication Trollope wrote to Longman: ". . . I suppose I may imagine that you do not consider the sale satisfactory." And a week later he announced, ". . . I should want a better price for another. . . . I am sure you do not regard £100 as adequate payment for a 3 vol. novel." When Longman refused his demand, Trollope found other publishers and in due course his books became best-sellers. The sales of *Barchester Towers* rose with his reputation, as is evidenced by large cheap editions in subsequent years. In its first format (1857) the book cost 31s. 6d.; a one-volume edition, priced at 5s., was issued in 1858; in 1866 the title was available for 3s. 6d.; in 1870 for 2s. 6d.; and in 1886 for 1s. His prestige, however, declined in the seventies, and reviewers began to say that his current work would not increase his reputation.

All his life Trollope held Barsetshire in affection. In 1881 he replied to a letter of praise: " 'Barchester Towers' was written before you were born. Of course I forget every word of it! But I dont. There is not a passage in it I do not remember. I always have to pretend to forget when people talk to me about my own old books. It looks modest. . . . But the writer never forgets." And he was pleased that same year when an American, speaking for thousands of readers, asked him to write another story of Barset. Though he felt physically unable to consent, he cherished the county he had created, and recounted the pleasure with which he saw published a collected edition of the Chronicles of Barsetshire.

The whole series retains today the cheerful sunniness which his contemporaries took for granted, but which we relish almost as an innovation. *Barchester Towers* possesses that amiable quality in great abundance, and yet, with the possible exception of Eleanor Bold's too easy tears, no trace of mawkishness will be found. On the contrary, satire is here in plenty—a satire that is always overlaid with warmth and sympathy and good humor. Trollope has added a pleasant place to those in which our lines have fallen; a good place, quiet but good, and one which it is a privilege to know.

Twenty years after writing the book, he described it in *An Autobiography* as "one of the novels which novel readers were called upon to read." This unassuming appraisal does scant justice to what has become a classic of nineteenth-century fiction. But though overmodest, his observation is as true now as when he made it: we are still called upon to read *Barchester Towers*, and there is no better time than the present.

The Morris L. Parrish Trollope Collection

It has been said of the Pre-Raphaelites that they tried to put into a picture of, say, a church, all that would be noticed by the worshipper, the architect, the priest, the tourist, and a person looking about the floor for pins. That they failed in reconciling these aims is a commonplace; but standards quite as diverse are met with complete success by the Trollope collection of the late Morris L. Parrish. It is the ideal of the scholar, the collector, the bibliographer, the bookdealer, and the person who merely wants to read Trollope.

This last-mentioned enthusiast is important, for in order to read much of this author it is necessary to collect him. Dickens, Thackeray, and many others are available in numerous complete editions; but no definitive set of Trollope has ever been published. It is only by laboriously assembling individual volumes that his entire works may be obtained—and some of them exist only in first edition form.

No one can appreciate the extent of Mr. Parrish's triumph except those who have tried to collect the first editions in their original state. It is not only a question of the money involved: there are at least a dozen titles which, in a decade of collecting, I have never seen offered for sale. Moreover, the average collector knows in what shabby condition certain books always turn up—and that, if he wants to be sure of a *Rachel Ray*, he had better seize the next rebound copy, and be content with it.

But in the Dormy House collection now housed in the Princeton University Library, it seems as though Trollope's publishers had wrapped up a copy of each work as it was

This appeared in The Princeton University Library Chronicle, *the November issue of 1946. That issue was devoted entirely to the Parrish holdings of various nineteenth-century English novelists.*

issued, and set it aside for Mr. Parrish. Practically everything is here, and practically everything is fresh, pristine, immaculate. And this, in spite of the fact that he used no case or protective jacket! He said, in an article which appeared in *The Colophon* twelve years ago: "I think, in the first place, that dust wrappers should be discarded the moment a book is received; than an unopened book has no place in any library, nor safes and vaults for the keeping of rarities. Cases, in my opinion, should be used only for volumes in wrappers and for pamphlets. A prominent collector, years ago, kept every book in his library in cases of similar color and design. To me, it is inconceivable that any true lover of his books should so hide them. Cases not only prevent one from seeing books in their original state, but when in variant bindings, make it impossible to distinguish them. If the object of the collector is simply to preserve his books for posterity, that is another matter; let us hope, however, that posterity will love the volumes enough to remove the cases."

At first it seems as though nothing would be necessary in the way of describing the collection but to quote from Mr. Sadleir's amazing bibliography. Yet even a casual examination shows that here there is enough material for a greatly expanded edition of that excellent work.

Let us look at a few items, although this method of attempting to skim the cream is always unsatisfactory. It must be understood that Mr. Parrish collected all variants, English *and* American, as well as the regular first editions. The three early novels, of which most collectors will never possess a copy, are all present: *The Macdermots* in crisp brown cloth, surely the finest copy known, *The Kellys* in cloth-backed boards (try to find such a one!), and *La Vendée* in two bindings—one in cloth-backed boards, the other in dark green cloth, presented to "M. A. Milton from the Author, June 11, 1850."

There are eight variants of the first English edition of *Orley Farm*, a major bibliographical puzzle; and they are an excellent example of Mr. Parrish's meticulous studies, since he listed their differences in binding, stab holes, endpapers, catalogues, and so on. A beautiful *Rachel Ray*, that black swan, is here; and besides all the regular issues of *Can You Forgive Her?*, a one-volume American edition in wrappers copied from those of the English part-issue.

There are three English firsts of *The Last Chronicle of Barset*, each with endpapers of a different color—white, yellow, and buff. No bibliographical detail was too small for Mr. Parrish: there are two copies of *British Sports and Pastimes*, one with, and the other without, a period after the name "Trollope" on the spine. This reminds me of an item Mr. Parrish did not own. *Ralph the Heir* has a curious publishing history: it was issued in parts, as a three-decker, and also as a Supplement to the *Saint Paul's Magazine*. Of this last issue Mr. Carroll Wilson possesses an astonishing copy—the title on the front wrapper has a comma, thus: *Ralph, the Heir*. I once mentioned this to Mr. Parrish, who observed with startling vehemence, "He's awfully proud of that comma!" Clearly he felt that this particular punctuation mark would have graced Dormy House.

He Knew He Was Right is here in the regular issues, as well as a variant binding with altogether different lettering and decoration. There is *An Editor's Tales* with no title or author's name on the front cover; there are two copies of *Sir Harry Hotspur* with circles of different sizes at the foot of the backstrip, a point not mentioned by Sadleir. There is an illustrated *Golden Lion of Granpere* (Tinsley, 1872) in *green* cloth with the lettering entirely unlike that of Sadleir's second (illustrated) issue.

The Eustace Diamonds appears in an unheard-of green binding with the author's name and the volume numbers spaced differently from the familiar first edition. There is a part-issue of *The Prime Minister* in tan paper wrappers, a *Cousin Henry* in green-ochre cloth, an *Ayala's Angel* in grayblue, a *Marion Fay* in blue-green—all of these being lusus naturae.

It is true that the ordinary reader or student will not find his primary interest in these matters, but he can appreciate the extent of Trollope's text, which is simply not available elsewhere. Mr. Parrish assiduously gathered all periodicals that contained stories or articles by Trollope, many of which were never reprinted. The author has much to say of the Civil Service in *The Three Clerks*, *The Small House at Allington*, and other novels; there is also a lecture on "The Civil Service as a Profession," included in the volume *Four Lectures by Anthony Trollope*, which Mr. Parrish edited; but few libraries besides this can show a copy of the *Dublin University Magazine* for October, 1855, which contains the earliest Trollope article on *Civil Service*.

We know that Trollope was interested in an international copyright law; and Mr. Parrish procured the *Transactions of the National Association for the Promotion of Social Science* (London, 1865), which contains Trollope's "On the Best Means of Extending and Securing an International Law of Copyright." Trollope dramatized *The Last Chronicle of Barset*, and, of course, there is a copy of the exceedingly scarce *Did He Steal It?* on these shelves. For those who remember the novel, I include here a partial list of the "Persons to be Represented," and add their original names where Trollope has changed them. It is interesting to note that the clerical atmosphere which gives the Barsetshire novels their color has been carefully expunged; apparently the stage was too vivid a medium in which to treat the Church of England with anything but awe.

 Josiah Crawley, a schoolmaster at Silverbridge.
 Mr. Goshawk, a magistrate at Silverbridge. (Bishop Proudie)
 Captain Oakley, son to Mrs. Goshawk,—in love with Grace Crawley. (Major Grantly)
 Mr. Toogood, an attorney from London, cousin to Mrs. Crawley.
 Mr. Thumble, the new schoolmaster.
 Mrs. Goshawk, wife of the magistrate. (A blend of Mrs. Proudie and Mrs. Grantly—which would have horrified that pair of enemies!)

An example of Trollope's periodical publication (1878).

Mrs. Lofty, benevolent old lady belonging to Silverbridge. (Mrs. Arabin)

These are but a few random choices from the great mass of ephemera that has been brought together. Of another sort, more important, perhaps, are the autograph letters which Mr. Parrish collected. There are nearly three hundred specimens of Trollope's correspondence, and transcriptions or photostats of many more. Their value as biographical material cannot be over-estimated. At the time of his death Mr. Parrish was planning to publish Trollope's letters, but that project fell to other hands.

The one category which is lacking is manuscripts. For some reason Mr. Parrish took no interest in them. This is a pity, for there is hardly a novel without some doubtful reading, some obvious error; and he would have done a scholarly job of collating the carelessly printed page with what Trollope actually wrote. Perhaps the explanation is that of course he could not secure all of the extant MSS. and he wished to have no incomplete group. Half measures would not have satisfied him.

But the novels themselves, whatever the state of their text, are a brilliant microcosm of Victorian life and manners; as Max Beerbohm says, Trollope was not "a mere interpreter of what was upmost in the average English mind: he was a beautifully patient and subtle demonstrator of all that was therein." And the social changes that he witnessed are reflected in his fiction; only consider the extent of the era that spreads between these two quotations:

". . . you'll see me yet, the gayest of the gay at Almack's . . . in twenty years' time; when I come forth glorious in a jewelled turban and yards upon yards of yellow satin—fat, fair, and forty."

"I have to meet five or six conservative members later on in the afternoon as to the best thing to be done as to Mr. Green's bill for lighting London by electricity."

Besides this detailed information of how a vanished age

acted and thought, the books and magazines form tangible evidence of the period's taste. From plain boards and labels to the most elaborately ornamented cloth, from the simple format of *The Life of Cicero* to the wedding-cake curlicues of *The Victoria Regia*, the changing styles and history of publishing are here for all to examine. The variant bindings and trial issues take on an added importance in this connection: they are part of the publisher's efforts to supply new and desirable products for the rapidly increasing number of readers.

The novels appear in one, two, three, and four volumes; they appear in weekly and in monthly parts, and there is even a double number of the first two parts of *He Knew He Was Right*, showing that a fortnightly issue was attempted. The influence of the lending library (which disliked the wrapped part-issues because of their fragility) made itself felt when the part-issue of *The Prime Minister* was made available in gray wrappers with or without a protective cloth binding.

Nor must the illustrations be forgotten, although Phiz, Millais, Marcus Stone, and the others are no longer names to conjure with. However, they faithfully reproduced their surroundings—and one of them contributed a tiny landmark to the history of book illustration: Stone's drawings for *He Knew He Was Right* were the first ever transferred by photography directly to the wood block for cutting. But their importance lies in the record they provide of costume and furnishings and all the particulars of the background. Indeed, so incomparably rich is the Parrish Collection that items like these, unimportant when isolated, here slip into place and assist in enlarging our knowledge of the period. The part-issue advertisements, for instance, describe objects used by Trollope's contemporaries—and (such is this novelist's power to convince us) we feel they were used by his characters also. Who would be surprised to find a notice mentioning Mr. Kantwise's iron tables and chairs in the *Orley Farm Advertiser*? Diligent search among similar pages may yet show us the "curious nettings" which were part of Griselda Grantly's trousseau, or perhaps Lily Dale's Balmoral boots.

For we are always fascinated by the trivia of earlier times; and rightly so, since these things make up the changing surface of all civilizations. As long as the panorama of Trollope's fiction retains any interest for posterity, these details will serve to swell and supplement this vast compendium of Victorian existence.

The Trollopes Write to Bentley

It was my good fortune recently to obtain a bundle of letters from four members of the Trollope family to the publishing firm of Richard Bentley. The letters range over a period of sixty-odd years, and are apparently only a random handful which has come to light out of what must have been an immense correspondence. Although, naturally, they are for the most part letters of business, they display so many of the family characteristics, including the positively Voltairean energy with which the Trollopes turned out such torrents of manuscript, that they merit attention.

Three letters of Frances Trollope begin the list:

My dear Sir

My kind friend Major Williams has undertaken to convey to your hands the first volume of "Paris and the Parisians" with the six plates and the vignette which belong to it—Mr Hervieu has still something to do to the plates belonging to the second volume.—Mr Trollope is still very unwell, but I trust that nothing will prevent my reaching London with the 2nd Vol about one week after you have received the first—I know that my M.S. is *now and always* so bad that it is hardly possible for any one but myself to correct the press—and I trust therefore that the proofs of the first volume will wait for me—

Tremordyn Cliff is particularly well printed which leads me to hope that the present M.S. may fare as well—I hope that you will give it the same printer as it appears that he is able to read my scrawl better than any other who has printed from it—It was my intention to have sent back to you the corrected copy—but the errata are so few as not to

This appeared first in the Trollopian, *now* Nineteenth Century Fiction, *Vol. 3, Nos. 2 and 3, 1948.*

make it worth while, and therefore I transcribe them—
Have the kindness to give Major Williams a copy of Tremordyn Cliff.—

                believe me truly yours

Chateau d' Hondt   F TROLLOPE
  Bruges
21st Oct 1835

The next letter is black-bordered:

My dear Sir

You will have probably seen by the papers that Mr Trollope is no more—He died the day after I had committed the 1st Vol. of my M.S. on Paris to the care of Major Molyneux Williams, who promised to deliver it to you.

This melancholy and unexpected event—for I believed all danger over—has rendered me very incapable of working—but my M.S. was so nearly finished that I trust it will answer your wishes—

I should be very much obliged my dear Sir if you would do me the favor of calling on me, to spare my going out—but if doing this should put you to any inconvenience I will call on you.—If however you can do me this favor, and will name the hour, either morning or evening, Mr Hervieu will be here to meet you, as he is desirous of being introduced to you—

I trust that you have received safely the M.S. and seven copper plates from Major M. Williams—The remaining seven plates were taken from us at Dover, but we hope to recover them at the custom house here.—

                Believe me dear Sir
                  truly yours

22 Northumberland St   FRANCES TROLLOPE
  Marybone
Saturday 7th Nov. 1835

The third letter is five years later, and dated from the house of her son-in-law, John Tilley, at Penrith, Cumberland:

My dear Sir

Will you have the kindness to tell me if the letter to Mr Haliburton which I took the liberty of sending to you some months ago, has been forwarded?—and also, what you consider as the best, and safest, mode of sending to him, either letters or parcel, without putting him to expense?

At length "The Ward," or, as I should greatly prefer its being called, "The Cousins," is ready for you; but notwithstanding the marvellous temtations [sic] offered by the penny post, I shall prefer conveying the M.S. to you by the hands of my son, who will give you a receipt for your nine months bill for £650 at the same time. Having completed the work coming out in Mr Colburn's New Monthly, I mean to start with my eldest son for Italy in a week or two, and as we shall make but one or two days delay in passing through London I will beg you to let me know whether you shall be in town about the 10th of next month, that no delay may arrive in getting your bill for "The Cousins,"[1] which I must negotiate before I start. One great reason for our being punctual to the time we have fixed is, that we have engaged to meet Madame Recamier, Lady Bulwer, and M. de Chateaubriand at Venice, in October—a brilliant knot, that it would grieve me to fail in promise to, even for a day.

                  Believe me dear Sir
                     truly yours

21 August 1840   FRANCES TROLLOPE

Next are eight letters from Anthony Trollope. The first is, so far as I am aware, the earliest one extant; and it is noteworthy that even in 1835 the urge for writing had begun.

My dear Sir

I called on you the other day at the request of the lady who is correcting the sheets of my Mother's work—The

---

[1] Despite her preference, Bentley published the novel in 1841 as "The Ward of Thorpe Combe."

Printers send the sheets very irregularly; in fact for the last Month I believe they have not sent any—of course you are the only judge of the time when the book is to appear, but perhaps you may not be aware of the dilatoriness of the Printers.

I now wish to trouble you on my own less important score—Is it in your power to lend me any assistance in procuring the insertion of lucubrations of my own in any of the numerous periodical magazines &c which come out in such Monthly swarms—I am not aware whether you are yourself the proprietor of any such—My object of course is that of turning my time to any account that I am able, and if you would put me into the way of doing so, & excuse the liberty I am taking you would much oblige
   My dear Sir
    yours truly
     ANTHONY TROLLOPE

Sunday 24 May 1835
22 Northumberland St.

The next letter is stained, and holes in the paper have damaged certain words, which are here supplied in brackets.

My dear Sir

I enclose a note from the lady on whose behalf I spoke to you the other day—to whom my Mother has entrusted the translation of her work on Austria into French—

If you will kindly read the accompanying letter [you] will perceive what she desires. Can anything be done in the matt[er?]

You would much oblige me, & confer a great obligation on Madame de Montalk—She wishes an assurance from you which she might shew to Soumier [?] that no one else would be enabled by you to translate the MS.—This is the chief thing—The next is that she might have the sheets of at le[ast] the 1st vol as they are printed—in the latter point if you are of opinion that it would be injurious, I would

not of course press you, but I could answer for their safety—
ever yours truly
Anthony Trollope

R B
16 Sept 37
Will you have the goodness to return the enclosed

The third letter refers to *The Kellys and the O'Kellys*; it is ten years later than the second, and all trace of his former diffidence has vanished.

Clonmel C° Tipperary
16 October 1847

My dear Sir

When in London in May last I spoke to you respecting a novel which I was then writing, and which I told you I should probably have finished in October. You said that if you published it, you would like to do so in November.

It is now all but completed—and I would wish to know at what time you would wish to publish it, if you do publish it.

I will *not part with the MS. on any other terms than that of payment for it*. I mean that I will not publish it myself—or have it published on half profits—or have the payment for it conditional on the sale. It is, and must be, much more the publishers interest to push a work when it is his own property.

If you wish it under these circumstances, I will send you the MS.—But I should be glad to know at what time you would think of publishing it. I could immediately send the MS. of the whole wanting about 60 pages—It may however be a month before I am able to complete it, as the opening of the Irish Railways take up all my time.

very faithfully yours
Anthony Trollope

Richard Bentley Esq
   Publisher
New Burlington St.

None of the Trollope family believed in the royalty system; Tom Trollope, as we shall see, still held the same attitude many years later. In this case, however, Bentley refused the novel after Anthony sent it to him.

> Clonmel October 30—1847
>
> My dear Sir
>
> I have sent the MS of my novel to you—by the hands of Mr Milton, who will deliver it to you. It wants four chapters of being complete. but [sic] I imagine you can judge of it now as well as if it were complete. I had an opportunity of sending it which I did not wish to pass over. The remainder will be ready at any time at which it may be wanted—
>
> faithfully yours
> ANTHONY TROLLOPE
>
> R Bentley, Esq

Another ten years pass, and he is writing quite crisply about *The Three Clerks:*

> My dear Sir
>
> I have received your note of hand & am obliged—amount £250
>
> I did *not* dispose of the copyright of B. Towers to Messrs. Longman—
>
> I do and will return the sheets to Messrs Woodfall and Kinder without delay of a post—I think there must be some mistake for they have sent me back today a lot of sheets, which I had corrected—or rather they sent me duplicate sheets, these duplicates *not* containing the corrections made by me.
>
> I cannot imagine why this has been done.
>
> Yours very truly
> ANT. TROLLOPE
>
> R Bentley Esq

We need only recall that Bentley would not meet Trollope's

terms for *Doctor Thorne* to appreciate with what satisfaction the following note was dashed off:

Cadiz 28 April 1858

My dear Sir:
   The day after I last saw you I sold the MS of "Doctor Thorne" to Mr Chapman. It will be published I believe in May
   I shall be in London soon, & I will then call on you.
faithfully yours
ANTHONY TROLLOPE

R Bentley
New Burlington St.
London

Dublin: 8 August 1859

My dear Sir
   Your letter of the 4th Inst has followed me here.
   When you were about to bring out your 5/– edition of the The Three Clerks, I reduced the book by about 60 pages, and I fear I should find it impossible to put out 100 more. It gives more trouble to strike out pages, than to write new ones, as the whole sequence of a story, hangs page on page—There is an episode—a story of some 40 pages in the three vol edit., which I would put out if that would suit you—But even that w^d require some care as it is alluded to in different places.
   I should not at all object to your midwifery for a new book. But as long as Mr Chapman will give me what I ask him for my goods, of course I shall continue to sell them to him.
very faithfully yours
ANTHONY TROLLOPE

R Bentley Esq

The last letter was written only seven months before Trollope's death, and refers, of course, to the never-completed *Landleaguers*.

Harting, Petersfield
March 30, 1882

My dear Mr Bentley,

I am going over to Ireland and shall bring out a novel as to the condition of the country,—which you will agree with me is lamentable enough. It will be in 3 volumes,—same length as American Senator,—and will be ready some time early next year. Would you like to have it for the "Temple Bar"—The price for the magazine will be £400. You can begin it when you please, but I should wish it to be published as a whole in 1883.

You can have it altogether if you would like it for £1100
Yours very faithfully
ANTHONY TROLLOPE

Richard Bentley Esq

The letters from Thomas Adolphus Trollope form by far the largest group in this collection. There are fifty-five altogether, too many to quote here; enough will be given, however, to indicate the quality of a literary career that never once slackened its furious pace for more than half a century. The first one begins with an echo of *The Domestic Manners of the Americans:*

Dover. Sunday. Sept. 16th, 1838

I hear from Mr Hervieu that you think of having a series of American drawings engraved by him, and publishing them with a couple of volumes post 8vo—and that you commissioned him to speak to me on the subject.

I have talked the matter over with my mother—and with the assistance she promises me, I think, that if you feel inclined to trust it to me, I can undertake it with some confidence.

My own recollections and journals will furnish me with sufficiently ample materials and my mother promises me the use of all her note-books—as well as the benefit of her perusal and corrections of the M.S.

As I am, and for some time past have been, engaged on an undertaking, which I hope to speak to you about at some future time—and which I must lay aside for the present if I undertake this American book, I should not be willing to work at it, unless certain of the result. On the other hand I am [sur]e than an untried author cannot expect any terms except such as an older hand would not dream of accepting.

Taking all this into consideration—I will write the two volumes post 8vo—to be read and corrected by my mother—for £150.—and if you wish it, the first chapter shall be submitted for your approbation before signing any agreement.

Thus the beginner. Here he is, thirty-one years later, as "an older hand," referring, perhaps, in the end of his letter to the very proposal mentioned above.

Florence. 9 Decr 1869
Villino Trollope

I am much obliged by your friendly letter of the 27th Nov^r.

The run to Florence is so quick and easy now that I will not give up the hope of seeing you here "on a long Vacation ramble" some day. Easy and quick in ordinary weather that is to say! For latterly we have been having weather which has made the Mont Cenis in a horrible state, thrown our posts all out of gear, and sent no end of hapless stray Bishops bound for Rome wandering about Europe in very uncomfortable and unepiscopal plight. Nevertheless, I suppose a letter and packet of M.S. which must have crossed your letter on the road must have reached you by this time. The M.S. is an account of the St. Medard Convulsionnaires, which I hope you may find interesting.

Austin and his wife had left us for Rome before your letter reached Florence. I mentioned in writing to him, that he would have a letter from you shortly.

As to what you mention about your owing me something on account of "Temple Bar," he will kindly put the matter right with you; as he was kind enough to arrange for the publication of the Articles.

Many thanks for what you say about books. Some day I shall tax your kindness, you may depend upon it. Miss Mitford was a very old or intimate friend of my mother; and I shall much like to see her letters. I shall hope to do something more for you for T. B. before long. But I have undertaken the Italian (not Roman) correspondence for the Times, and that takes more hours in the week, than you would perhaps imagine.

Pray remember me kindly to your father. I doubt though he will hardly remember the youngster who used to drive hard bargains with him some thirty-five years ago!

On the tenth of January, 1870, he writes:

This morning reached me safely, and "in good condition" as the bills of lading say, the books you have had the great kindness to send me. I have only seen the outside of them as yet; but that is sufficient to insure one's admiration for the elegant "get up" of both of them, specially of the Austin Memoirs. Mary Mitford was a very old—almost a life long friend of my mother's; and I shall have great pleasure in reading the memoirs.

Did you see a review of "Ouida's" "Puck" in the Pall Mall? and what did you think of it? There can be no doubt that it will very powerfully contribute to the sale of the book.

I am not altogether satisfied with the article on the "Convulsionnaires." It was somewhat too chopped-hay-like. That arose from the necessity for brevity. And perhaps after all you liked it better as it was, than if it had been somewhat better told in a greater number of pages. I hope very shortly to send you something better....

Ten days later he writes, as he did so often, apologizing for the length of his articles:

I do not like Ouida's novels a bit better than you do. What I meant to call your attention to in the review I mention'd was the very severe censure of the reviewer express'd nevertheless in such a form and manner as to contribute powerfully to the sale of the work.

I send you by this day's post the M.S. of an article for the T. B. You ask me for "a short Italian story of artist life," and if the story I now send had not been nearly written when I received your letter, I would have sent you something more nearly like what you desire. I will do so before long. The story I now send is, I think, not a bad one, and very characteristic of Italian life. *But* it has come to be longer than you will like it, and longer than I intended it to be. I think it would make nineteen T. B. pages, but I am afraid you will hardly allow me so much space. If you cannot put it in as it is, it might begin where I have put two crosses in red ink in the margin, in page 4 of the M.S. This would, I calculate, reduce the article to 17 pages.

If that is still more than can be tolerated, it might begin where I have put three red crosses in page 8 of the M.S. And this I think would reduce it to 15 pages.

Should this latter course be adopted the paper must begin with the sentence written in red ink in the margin of page 8 of the M.S. If this course is *not* adopted the pen must be struck through the passage in red ink.

If prefer'd the entire paper might be left as it is, and divided into half for two numbers of the magazine. In this case the division should be made where I have put four red crosses in the margin of page 19 of the M.S. And no change need be made for that purpose save introducing at the beginning of the Second Part the words I have written in red ink in the margin of page 19 of the M.S.

I am sorry to trouble you with all this; and will, I hope, not fall into the same abomination another time.

I have read the Memoir of Miss Austen. It is very pleasingly written, evidently by one who is both a sensible man and a gentleman. Is it not a striking fact that "Woodstock" should have brought its author £8000, while Pride and Prejudice only produced £150! I should think that the latter must sooner or later have produced as much to the publisher, as Woodstock.

My wife has been reading the Memoir of Miss Mitford with great delight; and I hope to do so. It is full of notices more or less interesting of persons whom I have known. What an old scamp her father was!

Will you kindly send the numbers of the T. B. which contain'd the article on "Ginevra Almieri" and that which contained "Jean Calas" for me to care of "Mrs. Ternan, 305 Vauxhall Bridge Road." Any cheque sent for me to Messrs. Woodhead and Co. 44 Charing Cross will duly go to my credit. But I should at any time be much obliged by a line telling me that any such payment has been made;—otherwise I shall know nothing about it, till the end of the year. . . .

P.S. If a portion of my M.S. be discarded I should be obliged by your sending it to me with the proofs; as the remarks made in the introduction are just;—and might be used elsewhere.

Florence, 2nd March, 1870
Villino Trollope

I send you herewith by the kind intervention of our friend Austin a short article, which I hope will answer to your desire to have something "of artistic life." Pray tell him what you have done with the story I sent you. He will let me know, and it will save you the trouble of writing. Miss Mitford's letters are delightful.

Florence. 9th March. 1870

I am much obliged for your letter of the 1st of this month telling me that you have paid £20 to Messrs. Woodhead on my account. Your statement of the account is about the mark I think.

Before this reaches you our friend Mr Austin will have handed you an article (short—about 10 pages) entitled "An

Artist's tragedy." It is on the story of Andrea del Sarto, and I think you will like it.

I shall send you another bit of artist life before long. And I should not have troubled you by writing till I did so, were it not for the sake of duly acknowledging the £20.

Florence. 6th April. 1870

By this day's post I send you for T. B. an article on "Fra Filippo Lippi." It will make a "pendant" for the one on Andrea del Sarto.

Will you kindly send me a copy of the April number with my Tuscan story in it.

My wife,—with whom if you would make a run out here in the dead time of the year next Autumn, I should like to make you better acquainted,—has suggested to me that when you asked me to let you have something of "artistic life" for T. B., what you had in your mind was rather something of the nature of my little story published now so many years ago, "La Beata,"—than such articles as those I have sent you on A. del Sarto, and Filippo Lippi. So I am now going to try a little story of artistic life for you of that kind.

May it run to two numbers?

Florence. 2nd June. 1870

I am sorry that you won't have my novel. I wonder whether your reason is the same that led my friend Mr George Smith to refuse it for the Cornhill. He would have had it for that Magazine, but that he was afraid of the incident of the Seduction. I thought I had touched that with so light a hand that the most fastidious would not have objected to it! The seduction in "Adam Bede" is ten to one more objectionable. However I dare say that I shall hear what the motives of condemnation were from Austin, when he is able to write in less hurry than he did merely to tell me of the rejection.

By this same post I send you a story of Artist life in Florence, such (I hope) as you asked for. It is founded on a real incident of recent occurrence.

[128]

I wish you would tell me which you like best for Temple Bar,—such articles as those on Andrea del Sarto, and Fillippo Lippi; or those more of the nature of a story such as that now sent, and the "Bit of Tuscan Life in the 17th Century." Will you come and have a look at us here next October,— the dead time of your London year: but the pleasantest month of the year in our Florence.

Florence. 25th Septr. 1870

I suppose our friend Alfred Austin is now "sitting down" with the Germans before Paris. And one of the consequences of that is that I am obliged to trouble you with matters of business between us, which he, when he was in England, used to have the kindness to transact for me.

There have been published in Temple Bar the following articles of mine.

"A Romance of Florence." Augt 1869 . . Pages 10
"The Story of Jean Calas." Septr 1869 14
"Convulsionnaires of St. Medard." Jany 1870 . . . 14
"A bit of Tuscan life in 17th Centy." Apr. 1870 . . 17
"An Artist's Tragedy." June 1870 11
"A very naughty Artist." July 1870 15

─────
Pages 81

The value of this, I suppose is £50. 12. 6
Out of this I have received   £25. 5
  Still due to me—   £25. 7. 6

If you would send a cheque for this sum to Woodhead & Co. 44 Charing Cross—and give me a line to say you have done so (as otherwise I shall not know it) I should be grateful.

I do not know whether the article "A typical Pope" in the Septr Number is mine or not. If it is, you ought to have sent it to me, ought you not? Verbum sap.

We are as you may guess in a great state of excitement

here; and though we are wont to get excited with very small matters, Europe will admit that this entry into Rome is not a small matter. But now we have got Rome, what are we to do with it? The question seems to be felt on all sides as one of very great difficulty. It is by no means certain that the Capital will be or can be removed to Rome despite all the cries of all the newspapers. Here at Florence we look with considerable equanimity on the matter as far as Florentine interests are concerned; it being the opinion of the most competent judges that Florence (save perhaps for the first year or so) will by no means suffer from the change.

Florence. 17. Octr 1870

Returning from an absence of a few days I find your letter and two copies of T. B. for September. Many thanks for the same and for the payment of £25. 7. 6—which squares our accounts up to the end of July 1870.

I *suppose* that the Capital of Italy will have to be moved from Rome. Every other man in Florence would tell you that it was quite certain that it will be so. But I am not *quite* sure. The difficulties in the way are very great and of a very perplexing nature. There is no doubt that it is the very strong & even passionate desire of the Italian people to have Rome for their capital. To my mind it is equally certain that it will be a *very* great mistake to place it there, for reasons which I gave at length several years ago in the Cornhill Mag. I have the certain knowledge that it was the opinion of Cavour that Florence would be the most desirable capital for the United Kingdom.

You say you suppose I should not grieve at the transportation of the seat of government. Assuredly as a quiet place of residence Florence would gain rather than lose by the change. But I am a holder of house and land & have to look at the matter from that point of view. But I find that the best opinions,—those of business men, and of large speculators and contractors—are that Florence will in no wise suffer as to the value of property. Curiously enough house property at Turin is now worth fully as much as before the capital was moved thence,

I see that I transgress'd considerably in the matter of space in "Paul the 3rd." And I fear that I have done so also in the story you have "Meo Varalla,"—which Austin told me was to be printed in October. I suppose its length prevented that. Can you not cut in two? In future I will take care not to exceed my tether. Austin is still at the Prussian Head Quarters before Paris. We hear occasionally from his wife.

My wife will gladly comply with your request to send an occasional article to T. B. Our recent excursion was to a very little frequented and very curious part of the "Maremma," and she thinks of sending you a notice of that.

Hotel Laguna. Riva degli Schiavoni
Venice
17th July. 1871

Thanks for your letter of the 13th and for paying £200 for "Dunston Abbey." I should be much obliged to you to send one copy to Austin;—one to Mrs Taylor, The Lawn, Oxford;—one to John Tilley Esq. G. P. O.—and one to Harry Trollope of Chapman and Hall's for his father. . . .

I still look forward with patient hope to the publication of the Magazine articles. Austin has explained to me that the *length* of the articles has been the cause of the difficulty. I will not so sin again.

My hand is shaking so that I can hardly write,—not from drink, but from extreme heat, which has, the last two days, come upon us in earnest, and of which I hope you may have your share, which it seems you greatly need.

Venice. 18 Augt. 1871

I learn from my friend Austin that you will *not* undertake to receive a novel by me for the T. B.; but that you will undertake to look at a novel sent by me for that purpose, and to give me £150 for the M.S. in case you should *not* think fit to publish it in the T. B. and to give me £350 for the M.S. in case you *should* publish it in the T. B. Do I state this correctly? I am willing to write you a novel on these terms and understandings. I have a novel half-written, which I have taken much pains with; but I am disposed to think that I could do something better adapted to the T. B. if I wrote with a special view to that. I have also a Venetian story "on the stocks"—the result of my stay here. But neither is that, as I suppose, exactly the thing wanted for the magazine. And perhaps it would be better that I should write you an entirely new story of English life (entirely *new* of course; but I mean new *to me*, as having nothing to do with either of those mention'd above.

Will you kindly give me ten minutes *at once* to let me know, whether I shall do this on the above understanding; and *when* you would want the M.S. for the T. B. and *how much* of the M.S. it would content you to see. . . .

I am trying to sell my villa at Florence; but shall in all probability be there all this Autumn, and shall be delighted to receive you there, if you will run out for a short holiday. I shall be there from the 21st Septr and if you come there immediately after that date, you might probably have Alfred Austin for your companion guest during a week of your stay.

Florence—28th Sepr 1871

Allow me to express my sympathy with you in the loss you have recently experienced, and my high respect for the veteran who has "joined the majority" after so long and so good a fight. My relations with him went back to a time when he was still a young man, and I but a stripling; and my recollections of those days are all of courteous consideration and liberal dealing. The last time I saw your father was at a literary fund dinner some four or five years ago,—the year that the Duc d'Aumale was Chairman,—and I confess that I then thought that he was a good deal broken.

Florence. Gunpowder Plot Day. 1871

You asked me in your letter to me at Venice for some

sketches of characters; and our friend Austin, the other day, speaking of what I had written for Temple Bar, impressed on me the necessity of making my papers *short*, assuring me that if I would send *short* articles he thought I might depend upon their being inserted *promptly*. I thereupon send you by this post such a sketch, not more than ten pages of the Magazine in length. Is it such as you wish?

You say in your last letter that you are indebted to Mrs Trollope for the insertion of *an* article. The MS. of her's that you have in your hands contains *two* articles. Austin told me that you, in complaining of the length of it, said that it was 50 pages of the magazine. This must be an error. I think you will find that the two articles together do not make more than 32 pages.

Meo Varalla, (who sees the light at last after his long, long sleep,)—that work of my younger days—is, I own, unconscionably long. But then I meant it for two articles. Reading it now, when I had forgotten all about it, to speak honestly, it does not seem to me a bad story.

You have still to pay me for an article published in September, 1870, entitled "A typical Pope,"—18 pages. And if you will send me a cheque for that, and for "Meo Varalla" *crossed*, it will be very welcome.

I thought November would be just the time to tempt you to run out here—Through the tunnel too! Is it too late to make a sudden start? We will make you welcome to the best of our power.

Tunnel, quotha! You would be some six or eight hours longer on your journey than before the tunnel was open!!!! Those accursed enemies of the human race, the French, *took off* the express trains, as soon as ever the tunnel was opened!!!!!! Austin will tell you about it. Really our press ought to notice so flagrant a case of lese-public.

Florence. 17. March. 1872

Thanks for your letter this morning received. Before the Mont Cenis tunnel was opened our London letters reached us on the 4th day (inclusive); now they *always* reach us on the 5th. Let us hope that no more attempts at improving the route may be made!

I feared "The Stilwinches" might not suit Temple Bar. It was intended for a novel of character. Had the novel when first "put on the stocks" been intended for the Magazine I might have had a better chance. I felt this so much That I hesitated whether I should not begin another for T. B. And I should certainly have done so, had not the time given me been very short for the purpose. And I thought that writing a book in hot haste would not have given the best chance either.—Perhaps some day I may try again!

You may have heard of the little boy, who when told by his father that when he—the father—died, all those woods and cornlands would be his, replied briskly—"But when will you die, papa?" Now my reply to your promise to send me £150 *when* the novel is published is of the same kind! *When will* you print it?

Mrs Trollope—(I too)—is delighted to hear that her paper on Lamb has pleased you so much.

You are about, you say, to read the paper I sent you in reply to your hint that you would like some sketches of "characters I had met with." Did you read it? If so will you tell me quite frankly if it answers to the sort of thing you had in your mind when you asked for it. I have for a long time had by me a second which I wrote "to follow" it. Will you have it? Would you like to have it?—like it sufficiently to use it at once—i.e. not lay it aside for months and months. Tell me, sans façons, and I will do accordingly.

Mrs Trollope is getting on with the article on Varnhagen. The subject is rich in interest.

Many thanks for your word about sending me some books.

Florence. 28th March. 1872

... The sheets of "The Stilwinches," which I have had the proofs of, are in the main very well printed; but there are a few errors, of which it is *very* necessary that the corrections should be attended to. I give the hint, moved by much former experience. Could not the printer get on a little quicker?

Florence. 6 April. 1872

Mrs Trollope is disappointed at not getting a copy of the Temple Bar, for this month with her article on Charles Lamb. You always used to send me a copy of the magazine in the days long ago, when there was any article of mine published.

It is many days since I have had any proofs of the "Stilwinches." When the proofs came one sheet per diem, I grumbled at the slowness, seeing that at that rate, you would not get the book out till far in the summer. Now—to punish me I suppose for my discontent, the printing has ceased altogether!

You told me in your last letter that you were *that day* going to read the M.S. of my article "Antonio da Pelago" sent you last summer. Did you read it? Did you approve it? If you did so, I suppose you will be thinking of printing it next year, and publishing it the year after! Only remember that I am getting a very old man, and have not many years before me!

Did Mrs Trollope's article on Varnhagen,*—"In the Rhineland, 80 years ago,"—reach you duly.

Ricorboli 10 Apr. 1872

I am very much obliged to you for the kind liberality of your offer about the money for my novel. But I do not need to ask you to send it to me just at present. I shall want it in the course of the summer, and will ask you to send it to me when the need comes. And the payment for the article on "Lamb" will most conveniently be made at the same time.— I hope there may be by that time other articles to be paid for!

---

* Karl August Varnhagen von Ense (1785-1858) German diplomat and man of letters.

I have seen all about the copyright association,—but I do not see that it is very likely to forward the matter very materially. It is certain however that there is a movement in the same sense on the American side. And many of the *best* (perhaps not the largest) publishing houses are favorable to it. Harper the arch-pirate, I believe opposes all change—et pour cause! And I am told that the Philadelphia publishers—for some reason, which I don't comprehend—are strongly opposed to giving English authors or publishers any copyright in America. I have always thought that an English author might treat the matter on the same principle that "the Prophet" followed in his prohibition to eat pig. He forbad that a certain part of the swine should be eaten, without specifying *what* part. The good Moslems therefore are obliged to abstain from the whole animal, for fear of eating the tabooed part. Now suppose an English author were to cause *a* page of his book to be written by an American citizen. He would state that a certain part of his M.S. was copyright in America, as the work of an American citizen. Then, if any publisher in stealing his book, stole also *the American page*, he would be down upon them for piracy!!!!

What on earth were our medical authorities dreaming of to let the P. of W. go to Rome of all places in the world on recovering from typhoid fever? It is about the last place in Europe he should have gone to under such circumstances. However he is here now, and I believe all right. . . .

Your letter was unpaid. I tell you of it, because the probability is that some person, who ought to have paid it, robs you of a sixpence, & therefore probably of other sixpences, while robbing me of a shilling.

P.S. On looking again I see that there is a *fourpenny* stamp on your letter. The postage is sixpence.

As an improvement on my scheme for securing American copyright why should not an English author have an American "collaborateur" french fashion. "Blood and Thunder" A novel by A. B. (Englishman) and C. D. (American) stands on the titlepage. The *collaboration* is to be course *genuine*. But you will observe that a general revision of the punctuation would suffice for the purpose.

Florence. 19. May 1872

I send you herewith a third article by Mrs Trollope, completing the series on Varnhagen. Mrs Trollope is aware that at first *two* articles only were spoken of. But the interest of the subject is such and the matter so rich that she has been tempted to send you a third,—which you will accept or reject as you may think fit. My notion is that you will find this third paper to be the best of the three.

I shall want to draw on you, according to the permission you so kindly gave me, for the £150 for "The Stilwinches" in the early days of June. The price of Mrs Trollope's articles will have to be added to the amount. Will you be so good therefore as to calculate it, and let me have a line—*at once* as I am about to leave Florence for the summer—telling me the amount due to me, for which I may draw.

Rome March 12th, 1873

... I have never seen a copy of "The Stilwinches." It is too late now to make it worth while to ask you to send any copies for me to friends, whom I might have liked to see it. But I should still like to have one copy for myself. And now what can I say about the unfortunate articles written at your request for Temple Bar more than two years (!) ago? I have asked you again and again if they were unsuited to the magazine; and have had either no answer, or an answer in the negative. Indeed after you had seen them, you told our friend Alfred Austin that you would be willing to receive from me seven or eight such articles in the year. But . . . One such, a third written to follow the two you have, is now in my desk. Surely it would be better to publish these unhappy papers *at once* or *at once* to return them to me. Consider how very much more they must have cost me in annoyance, in disappointment, and long suffering, than in the trouble of writing them! Consider how very inadequate the shillings per page, which pay the latter, are to the payment of the former!

My wife tells me that you would like a novel on Roman life from me. The subject is rich and ample. I am thinking about it. Also of your other suggestion made to her—"Thirty years recollections of Florence."

21 Decʳ 1875 9 Via S. Susanna Roma

Thanks for your cheque for a "Ride across the Apennines." How true are the words of the sacred writer,—if you cast your bread on the waters you shall find it again after *many days!*

Thanks also for your kind word about my wife's forthcoming novel (which ought to be forthcome by this time). I am glad to see that my brother is going to give you a story for Temple Bar. His "Way we live now" was a charming book to us exiles from our country—so very consolatory! Upon my life you must have become a delightful set of people since I knew the manner of living in your little village!—at least if there is truth in Anthony's picture. . . .

Freihof. Baden. Switzerland. 3ᵈ Sepᵗ 1876

. . . Your observation in reply to my objection to the offer of a contingent sum in payment for M.S., that you "wish I had more faith in my book," is one that has been made to me before in similar circumstances, and that seems to smite the objector on the hip. Nevertheless I cannot admit that it does so. I *have* faith in my book. I think the subject an attractive one; and I think that the success of other works of the like kind gives me the right to think that I am capable of executing it satisfactorily. But I hold that an agreement that a publisher shall pay a given sum on the sale of a given number of copies, to be an essentially bad one, looked at in a commercial point of view. It places the interests of publisher and author necessarily in opposition to each other. We will suppose you to have sold 580 copies. The sale of the remaining twenty would put (say) eight or nine pounds into your pocket, *but* would cause you to pay £25—i.e.

some £15 or £16 dead loss on the sale of the twenty copies. If indeed you could be *sure* of selling the next two hundred, it would be worth your while to sacrifice this £16, together with another £25, in order to net about £80. But here again the sale of the last few copies of the 800 would entail a dead loss. Have I succeeded in making my meaning clear?

For these reasons, and not because I have no faith in my book, I object, not especially on this occasion, but on all occasions, to agreements framed on this plan.

Nevertheless since you will not come over to me, I must come over to you. You shall have the M.S.—about ninety thousand words, equal to a volume and a half for the terms you mention.

Please to cause agreements for this and for Mrs Trollope's novel to be drawn up and sent to me here. We shall be here for about the next three weeks.

This is a sleepy hollow sort of a place, very good to rest in for a while, for those who are disposed to rest and be thankful for it. . . .

P.S. Of course I sell you only the copyright for England and our colonies.

367 Via Nazionale. Rome.
29 Oct. 1876

Thanks for the letter with the agreement. I have copied and herewith send you the agreement for the Life of Pio Nono, duly signed. I have made two small alterations. Your copy says "Which is to form two volumes of the ordinary size of the volumes of the day." As there is no intention that it shall form anything of the sort, I have altered to "which is to contain the quantity of letterpress of two volumes" etc. Secondly in the clause about foreign rights I have added to the words in America the words "or elsewhere", thinking that Tauchnitz, who has occasionally reprinted other works than novels might possibly think it well to print a book *sure* of a large sale on the Continent.

It has broken my heart to copy all the useless verbiage of the agreement. I could put it in half the words! . . .

367 Via Nazionale. Roma
5th Dec.ʳ 1876

I think you have misunderstood what I said in my last letter, probably from my having imperfectly expressed my meaning. I did not apprehend that there was any misunderstanding between us as to the quantity of matter of which the Life of Pio Nono is to consist. I knew, and was aware you knew that it was to contain an amount of matter equal to two novel volumes. But the agreement spoke not of a quantity of matter *equal to* two novel volumes, but of the two volumes. Now I had supposed that we had agreed that the book should be in one volume such as my "Paul the Pope and Paul the Friar."—If you wish it to be in two volumes such as novel volumes, I will not object, in as much as I think you must be a better judge of the expediency of that than I am. For myself however I still think the one stout volume the better.

When I was with you in Burlington Street you sent off an article of mine to be printed for Temple Bar *Seance tenant* . But I have seen nothing of it in print. When is it to appear. I hope not "after a time and times" as the Apocalypse hath it.

367 Via Nazionale. Roma
2. Jany. 1877

It strikes me that you would do well to announce the "Life of Pius the Ninth." It is a subject which is *very* likely to be taken up. I am getting on well with it; and *hope* that it will be ready for press by the end of May;—but do not *promise* that.

Are you ready with "Black Spirits and White"? I take it the time you specified for the publication—five weeks before its conclusion in the "Graphic"—will be close at hand by the time this reaches you.

Do you remember sending out an article of mine for Temple Bar to be printed, while I was sitting with you? I thought to myself, "Well, there will be no delay *this* time!"

Will you, please, have the pockets of the man, who should have carried it to the printer, searched. I am afraid my M.S. must have remained in the recesses of one of them.

Very many happy new years to you! We are having lovely weather here, but our Carnival is to be a very dull one, by reason of the death of the King's daughter in law, the Duchess of Aosta. And strangers are few this year. . . .

Mrs Trollope sends you the "compliments of the season", and hopes you will send her a copy of "Black Spirits and White".

Geneva. Poste Restante
5th July. 1877

I have been very much pained and more astonished at the contents of a letter which you have written to Mrs Trollope about my life of Pius the Ninth.

You say it is "a great pamphlet", and I have not the least notion what is the idea in your mind, which this is meant to express. You say, I ought to have "approached it with a more artistic eye". Is there, in candour, *any* meaning in that at all? You say that I ought to have taken more time about it. Here we come to facts! In the first place you have not the smallest idea how much time I have taken for it. And in the second place, one man's labour for an hour and another man's labour for the like time may mean very different things. I wrote a novel in two volumes, which had a very fair success, in 24 days. If you can find another man alive who can do the like, I should like to see him. But the truth is that the time I have given to the subject is in no wise to be measured by the months which have expired since I spoke to you of it. My mind has been full of it for years. Lastly you say that the first paragraph in the book is "bad artistically" and "will predisdose [? predispose] the critics against it";—a most wonderful piece of criticism! Unluckily I have not here the means of referring to the proofs, and I do not recollect what this damning first paragraph was. But this I know, that the book was most conscientiously written, and . . . come! Since you compel me to defend myself, I will say, what I am *quite* sure of, that *no one who is at all likely to do it*, can give you a truer or more complete picture of the man. If what you have in your mind, is that the book should have consisted of an account of the Pope's private life and daily doings in the Vatican, no such book can or will be given to the world; or would have any value if it could. I *know* that I have written carefully, thoughtfully, impartially, with an eye to the great and permanently important issues which are and will be modified by the incidents of the Pope's career and the idiosyncrasy of the man. The book is NOT a bad book, say it who may!

My only critic, while it was in M.S., was my wife. She was much pleased with it. She is not a fool or illiterate; and I KNOW,—though you will naturally doubt it,—that I had her unbiassed opinion. You add to your condemnation that you will sell very few copies. I am persuaded that such *will* be the case. As I have very little hope of that patient, whose physician is convinced that he will die! Of course the book is foredoomed to failure whose publisher has conceived such a prepossession in its disfavour.

In nearly forty years of not unsuccessful authorship such an incident as this has never happened to me before. And I am amazed and greatly troubled by it.

48 Via Firenze. Roma
[Undated, but marked in pencil:
"rec^d 5 Dec 1886"]

I am sorry to see by your letter of the 22nd which reached me on the eve of my departure for Rome, that it will not suit you to take a novel from Mrs Trollope.

With regard to the "Octogenarian's Remeniscences" [*sic*] of which I spoke to your son, when I had the pleasure of seeing him in London I should like to hear your views upon the subject. I asked your son, what he thought should be the extent of such a book;—2 small vols post 8vo?—one stout vol demy 8vo?

He said but what could you make it?

But in truth I could fill a dozen volumes! The question is rather from the publisher's point of view, what the market would best bear? What exent would be most likely to succeed commercially? Your son seemed to think two vols demy would be desirable.

Now I am at work, and should like to have the benefit of your opinion, before the proportions and scale of the work are fixed.

Many thanks for Mad^e Galletti's book. It is bright and amusing, and as true as a photograph;—as I can testify.

48 Via Firenze. Rome
12 Decr 1886

Your letter respecting my proposed volumes of "Reminiscences" reached me yesterday.

With regard to the extent of the work, I recognize the expediency of making that a publisher's rather than an author's question. But my wife and other friends are strongly opposed to my limiting myself to the two small post 8vo volumes which you suggest. And it seems to me desirable before implicitly accepting your judgment on the point, to put before you a little (tho' very imperfectly) the variety of matter of which I have to treat. With this view I enclose you a sort of little synopsis—which I shall be obliged to you to return.

As regards your proposal that I should submit a portion of the work for inspection before any price is offered for it, I must say that I think it comes half a century too late. When you were in the cradle, or thereabouts, I should no doubt have acceded to a similar suggestion from your father. But after about forty eight (!) years of not altogether unsuccessful authorship I feel that it is rather *infra dig.* When Colley Grattan was proposing to me to visit him at

Boston shortly after the publication of my mother's book on America he said, "But if you were to come under a false name I think it would be *infra dig.* and yet if you come under your real name, you may very likely be *in for a dig!*"

Now I don't suggest the same alternative in the present case; but I think this examination business is rather for tyros than veterans.

Au reste—the paper I enclose will give you some idea of the nature of the matters which are to be "farrago Atelli."
P.S. My own notion was two vols demy,—400 pages each 250 words to page or thereabouts.

48 Via Firenze. Roma.
20 Decr 1886

Thanks for your letter, and your offer.

All right, I will complete the "Reminiscences" I am writing, in two volumes octavo, and accept from you for the same £300, with the understanding that I am to receive a farther sum of £200 when the sale shall have reached (if it should reach) 1500 copies.

But I should like to reserve to myself anything that I might be able to get from America, and to have your promise of your assistance in the furnishing of early sheets, in case I should be able to get an offer for them.

There would be but little to be got in this way; and I suppose you would not care much to look after it.

I mean to do the work, as well as I can; and to this end I must not hurry myself. I hope the M.S. may be ready to go to press next July. It will not be ready before.

You have not returned to me the little synopsis I sent you. Please do so. If you care to refer to it, as a diner looks at the menu put by the side of his plate, make one of your people copy it.

P.S. I did not mention in my menu that I shall have a few good letters from Landor, Dickens, G. H. Lewes, Geo. Eliot, Mrs Browning.

P.P.S. It occurs to me to mention another matter. I have

always objected to payments to author to be made "on the day of publication". It should be "on delivery of the M.S. in complete state for press". It is unreasonable that the author should wait for his payment till an event occurs which is wholly beyond his control, and wholly at the pleasure of the publisher. I do not mean that *you*, who have on other occasions treated me so handsomely, would do otherwise upon this occasion. But the rationale of the matter is, I thing, as I have stated it.

48 Via Firenze. Roma
2 Jany. 1887

Your suggestion of payment six week after delivery of the M.S. wholly meets my objection as to the "Greek Kalends" possibilities of the other arrangement, and is accepted nem. con.

I will do my best as regards the "cameo portraits", you speak of. If I do not succeed, it will not be for want of the "Capacity of taking trouble".

Thanks for falling in with my wish respecting American rights—or wrongs, as it may turn out. I shall I trust see you before the time comes for making any arrangements with regard to that matter.

Bon capo d'anno a Lei e tutti suoi.

Grand Hotel Sestri Ponente.
Presso Genova
3 March 1887

Thanks for your letter enclosing copy of the agreement, with my "rider" duly signed, which reached me here yesterday. "A Chapter on comparative manners—say of 1837 and 1887—would be very interesting [;] another on the London you first saw and the London of today", you write.

Excellent both. But in all that I have written of my early years, I have endeavored constantly to point, as I go along, the differences in social life, manners, and institutions. This is a main point in the "reminiscences" of one who is writing of 77 years ago!

You tell me not to "forget sketches or full length portraits of all the various eminent characters I have seen". This is (to use the slang of the day) rather "a large order". But I will do my best. I am at this moment attempting to give form to my remembrances of George Eliot and Lewes, of whom I saw much in Italy;—as well as subsequently in England.

With regard to Mrs Trollope's novel *perhaps* it may suffice you to see her first volume; and *perhaps* I may persuade her to shew it to you when it is completed. But she feels that she has sufficiently earned her spurs to make such a demand out of date. What a publisher (as it seems to me) has to go upon, is the fact, that all her former novels have contented the publishers of them; and as she does not ask any higher terms than she has had for her preceding works, there is every reason to anticipate that, the present book equally satisfy its publishers. . . .

Heath Cottage. Hothfield
14 Sep 1887

I am much pleased to hear that you find "What I Remember" amusing.

I have looked at the passage you refer me to,—"sharp practise". I do not think that we need trouble the printer with any alteration. Mr Sloane and his widow, childless, have long since gone over to the majority. Besides I charge them with no sharp practise. I say that I believe the other parties imagined themselves to have been so treated. It is the fact that they did so imagine. They also have quitted the scene. Moreover I say, that I have no knowledge of the rights of whatever dispute there may have been.

If you think it worth while, the words "unhandsome treatment" may be substituted for "sharp practise". If you do think it worth while, please order the printer to make the change.

I have had no made up sheets since page 128 Vol. II. All

that I have had since, some 80 pages or so, has been sent on slips. If they would send me some *sheets* (which must be sent for the page headings) I could be getting on with the Index for the 2nd Vol. That for the first Vol. has been done and sent up to them.

Heath Cottage
24 Sep. 1887

I have this morning your letter to Messieurs Clay pointing out the astounding blunder I have made respecting the death of the Irish duellist at Lucca Bath.

I am amazed and not a little ashamed of the incredible carelessness which could print "Whether he is alive or not I do not know" of a man whose death I saw, and whose death I was relating!!!

It is extraordinary that this passage should have passed *three* other readers besides myself,—my wife, my sister in law and her husband—without detection;—not to mention the corrector of the press. Of course the matter does not come within the scope of his strict duties; but he has kindly noticed several other matters far less startling.

What should I do without a publisher who does something more than merely *publish*? I am much your debtor for the correction. You say mildly that the statements in the text are "contradictory". Rather so! Even the "general reader" might have noticed a slight inconsistency!

I have told the printer to alter the words following "print his name" on page 141 to "He has gone to his account. But it might nevertheless happen that the printing of my story with his name in these pages might still give pain to somebody." This change will necessitate but a small displacement of type.

I shall be ready with the M.S. of the Index to the 2nd Vol within 24 hours of receiving the last proof sheet.

I have sent the printer a few lines of dedication to be printed at the beginning of the book, which I hope you will not disapprove. I dedicate the work

"Omnibus Wiccamicis."

P.S. Yours of the 23 just to hand. What is your "grazie" mistake to mine! about the man killed in a duel.

Yes! I fear that the foreign part of my book is necessarily less interesting to English readers. But I hoped that many of the letters I give might be deemed valuable,
P.S. Sunday morning.

I am distressed to find by the last sheets of my second Volume received this morning that the printer has *again* misled me as to the length of the M.S. I do not know whether the matter has been brought to your cognizance, but Mʳ Richard Bentley knows all about it. After their *first* blunder they told me that the M.S. for the second volume extended to 376 pages. I set to work immediately and supplied matter by interpolation, partly in the sheets already printed, and partly in the M.S. not yet set up to the extent of 17 pages bringing the volume up to 393, which with the Index would have turned the 400 pages. I now find that the printed volume makes only 379 pages. The Index will make, perhaps, 15 or 16 more. It is very vexing. Had I not been deceived by the first miscalculation I could readily and easily have made the M.S. extend to 800 pages for the two volumes. You can judge better than I can how far this falling short may be supposed to be prejudicial to the book. I did my best to remedy the first error; and might perhaps find the means of remedying this second mistake; but at the cost of considerable loss of time and *much* dislocation of type. I am sending to the printer matter for a couple more pages.

Cliff Corner, Budleigh Salterton, South Devon
31 July 1888

You are not very encouraging. Doubtless all that you say against "continuations" is true, and strong in favour of "sansculotism". Quite true that it cost as much to advertize a work in one volume, as one in twenty. However we will "see about it". But when you cut down an author's terms, I think you ought to *come* and tell him so. A run down here—six hours, all told—in the silly season would be "seasonable" and do you a world of good. You should have a bedroom with a look out over the sea, and we would make merry over a sparkling glass of . . . Apollinaris.

Won't *that* tempt you? Give us a line to say when we may look out for you.

P.S. Look at my wife's novel "That Unfortunate Marriage", now coming out in the Graphic, with a view to giving me an answer when I come to you about the book publication of it. It is one of the best stories, she has written,—if not *the* best.

Cliff Corner, Budleigh Salterton, South Devon.
1 May. 1889

I reached home last night, and send you at once, as we arranged, the photographs of my villa near Florence; the photographs, of Mrs Trollope; and a water-coloured drawing of myself when young.

You will see which of these (or whether any) will be available for the 3rd Volume of "What I Remember".

Of the photographs of my Villa the first one will shew you my house marked "a"—and Rusciano, mention'd in my book, an historical villa inhabited by Fenzi, my nearest neighbor.

The prettiest bit is that marked "5", shewing part of the garden front.

That marked "8" shews the hall, and some marble columns, which came from the cathedral, and which are mention'd in the book.

Please return what you do not intend to use.

Cliff Corner, Budleigh Salterton, South Devon.
25. June. 1889

I have received today a printed form from New Burlington Street, informing me that Proof Sheets of Vol III of "What I Remember" will shortly be forwarded to me.

This looks as if you were not aware that the first three

sheets were sent to me long ago,—so long ago that it would seem as if the printer also had forgotten all about it. Why do they not go on? I see however on looking at the back of the printed notice that it must have been sent to me because specially needed!

It is addressed to "an Author on passing a first work through the press"!! Alas! You have begun at the wrong end of me! I had dealings with Richard Bentley more than half a century ago—in 1835. I should think I must be the oldest client on the books of the firm!

It is gratifying however to see that you consider me to be evidently at the beginning of a long career!

Of the letters of Frances Eleanor Trollope, Tom's second wife, some are interesting in their own right, and others because they mention her husband and his family. And in them all is evidence of how completely she absorbed the Trollope attitude towards writing and publishing. The earliest from which I quote is dated:

The Lawn, Oxford.
Saturday November 2nd 1872

... I should much like to do a little paper on Florence for your magazine, and I think you yourself have suggested a good title for it "the City of Lilies". But I do not yet quite see my way clearly to it. I have to be peculiarly careful in writing about Florence, as many of the figures which would give piquancy and freshness to a little water colour sketch of the place, belong to my personal acquaintance. And when the city is mentioned by name, it is a little like walking on eggs to attempt a sketch of it. Of course one could leave the people out altogether. But then a landscape without figures—! If you will allow me, I will think the matter over....

Decr 28th 1872
The Lawn, Oxford

I forward by this post a paper for Temple Bar, entitled

(in your own words) 'The City of Lilies'. I should have sent it before this time, but wanted to procure quite accurate data for the story of Bastianini. I have done the article con amore, and hope you will like it. Of course, as we all know who understand the practical working of our calling, and the limits of time and space to which all artists have to submit their conceptions, the trouble in such a paper is not what to say, but what to leave unsaid.

My husband seems to take kindly to your suggestion about the reminiscences of Florence. His thirty years residence there, and his knowledge of—one may say without exaggeration—*all* the interesting figures who have appeared on that scene within his experience of it, ought to furnish a book of very general interest. I wish Mr Trollope were here to talk it over with you. But I fear there is little chance of his coming to England at present. I must not forget that he bade me ask you if you thought of using some papers he sent you some time back about one or two Tuscan oddities. One, I remember, was on Antonio da Pelago. If you do not think they can be made available for the magazine, will you kindly have them forwarded hither to me? . . .

The Lawn, Oxford
Sunday night, Jany. 26th 1873

My husband wrote to me the other day, calling my attention to an article in the 'Athenaeum', in which mention is made of the works and autobiography of the German poet and dramatist, Grillparzer. . . . Mr Trollope thinks, and I think too, that a bright & interesting paper might be written for 'Temple Bar' on the autobiography. . . .

If you think that a paper such as I have mentioned, would be acceptable for 'Temple Bar', I will ask you to let some of your people procure the works & autobiography for me, at trade price, before I leave England. . . . I have further, by Mr Trollope's request to ask a favour. Will you kindly cause to be brought for me at trade price, Greg's 'Enigmas of Life', in one volume, Trübner & Co.? My husband tells me he has been reading the book with the greatest interest and admiration, and wishes to possess it. We have just sold a library of ten thousand volumes, and here we are beginning to collect again! But what is to be done? One may live without butter to one's bread, but not without books! I shall feel much obliged to you, if you can without inconvenience comply with this request. . . .

I am in daily expectation of receiving my marching orders. After much debate, we have come,—unwillingly, I own—to the conclusion that my stepdaughter, Miss Trollope, cannot safely be made to reside in England all the year round. So for the present we must continue to make Italy our headquarters. This being the case, Mr Trollope has accepted the post of "own correspondent" to the "Standard" which has been offered to him, and we shall pitch our tent in Rome. I wish that 'pitching our tent' were indeed no metaphor, for the difficulty and expense of finding a dwelling in the Eternal City are very great indeed. However, Mr Trollope will go thither in a week or so, and I shall join him there.

I must not omit to remind you once more of the Italian papers which my husband wrote for T. B. at your suggestion, and which you told our friend Austin, you considered acceptable. Otherwise I shall be scolded for neglect of orders!

3 Via Rasella, Rome.
February 3^d 1874

You told me when last I had the pleasure of seeing you, to direct my steps to No. 8 Burlington St. when next I should have a substantive word to dispose of. A three volume novel of mine is to be begun in "All the Year Round", at the beginning of /75. What terms can you offer me for the subsequent copyright of it? It is a story of English domestic life. You will understand that it is important for me to get your answer as quickly as possible.

I do not know whether, when you spoke to me, you

meant that I should try my hand at a novel for 'Temple Bar'? But if that were your intention, I should be happy to make the attempt on a future occasion. My old connection with 'All the Year' led to the publication of this story in their columns....

Wharton House, Margate
June 22^d 1877

Do you think you are likely to accept a novelette of mine, making about one novel volume of three hundred pages, for 'Temple Bar'? I have it with me, and should like you to see it. To say the truth it was begun last winter with the idea of giving it to the "New Quarterly" the editor of which has published a short story of mine and asked for another. But I found that my picture was somewhat too big for the canvas they could afford me, and rather than spoil my subject I finished it in its present form, and it is a very nice story though I say it!!

If you choose to take it merely to pass it through 'Temple Bar' leaving me the right of republication, you shall have it at magazine price. Will you let me have a line in reply addressed to my brother-in-law's house 39 Montague Square? I am going up to town tomorrow to stay over Sunday and say 'good bye' to Anthony before he starts for Africa. I made a sudden rush to England leaving Mr Trollope in Rome. We are to rejoin each other in Switzerland early in July.—If you think of taking my story and can make room for it *soon*, I will send it to you. But it would not be worth my while to wait a twelve-month for its publication. A month or two would not matter.... In writing to Montague Square please address me Mrs T. A. Trollope, otherwise my sister-in-law will naturally open the letter.

Rome. 48. Via Firenze
December 12th 1886

I should like very much to write a novel for you, and hope to do so. Since Mr Trollope saw you in London, I have undertaken to write a 3 vol. novel which has another destination, and I am now, in fact, engaged on it. I think I understand from your letter, that what you would wish would be a novel which had not previously appeared in serial form? I have in my mind the idea of a story which would run to about the length of two ordinary novel volumes. At your leisure you can let me know whether such a length would be at all likely to suit you.

I have looked over the summary my husband has sent you, and am struck at once by its—no doubt inevitable—incompleteness! At once half a dozen names come into my mind about the owners of which he has something more or less interesting to say:—Our lamented Princess Alice whom we met at Sir Augustus Paget's house in Rome, and to whom Mr Trollope was presented at her request, Lord Houghton, with whom he lunched shortly before his death, Charles Lever, whom he knew well at Florence, Longfellow who came to our house at Florence, Garibaldi, ditto ditto,—in short a procession of distinguished and interesting figures. Our friend 'George Eliot' used frequently to urge my husband to set down his reminiscences, not only of persons, but of manners; deeming it, as she said, very important to preserve the continuity of our social history by means of individual memory. With her pious attachment to the past, and her compassionate affection for those whose lives and struggles have prepared and lightened our own, you can easily understand that she attached a great deal of weight to a record which she was well persuaded would, to say the least, be a *true* one.

Rome. 48. Via Firenze
Tuesday December 21st 1886

Thank you very much for your letter, which enables me clearly to understand the reasons in favour of 3 vols. *versus* 2 vols. The only thing to be done, is to endeavor to lay out one's story so as honestly to fill a bigger canvas, without too much mere talkee talkee. People who have only struck ink and not oil, must consider the profit question: whether they have to deal with the article in the oily form of printer's-ink, or the thinner liquid fresh from its native bottle. So it is evident that both publishers and writers must for the present stick to the three volumes.

I hope and expect to have the M.S. of a novel ready by the spring of *1888*. Could you tell me—supposing I have life and health to carry out this intention—what sort of price you would be prepared to offer for a 3 vol. novel which should not previously have appeared in any periodical? ...

P.S. We are intending to make a three months tour in Spain (including, probably, Gibraltar, and a glimpse of Tangiers) during March, April, & May 1887. Do you think a series of papers from Spain, written as brightly as circumstances (over which I have no control!) will permit, would be acceptable to Temple Bar, with a view to subsequent publication in a volume?

86 Sutherland Avenue W
December 23^d 1894

Since I saw you I have been looking over a great mass of papers relating to Frances Trollope. There is a vast deal of great personal interest to the family, and, I think, a considerable amount of matter calculated to amuse the public. But it will take much *boiling down*. I am spending Christmas in town with my own people. When I return to my Berkshire cottage,—which will be I reckon early in the second week of January—I shall endeavor to draw out and send to you a little sketch of the materials at my disposal. I am very anxious to procure if possible, some letters that passed between Mrs Trollope and her husband before their marriage. You may possibly remember that Anthony alludes to them in his autobiography as having been sent to him anonymously. Anthony gave them to his brother; and after my dear husband's death, I gave them to Henry Trollope, Anthony's eldest son. Henry Trollope is at present in Switzerland and is not likely to be back in England for some time to come. Were he in London I dare say he would permit me to use them. But I greatly fear that these letters may be packed and stored in some (to me) inaccessible repository, since H. Trollope has given up his London house. I will write to him at once on the subject, and let you know the result. So far as my memory serves me the letters in question contain scarcely any facts essential to the Memoir of Frances Trollope, but they afford a pleasant glimpse into the form and manner of an old-world courtship.

I cannot refrain from saying that, high as my respect for "The Mammy" (as we always spoke of her en famille) has been ever since I first heard or knew anything of her, it has been enormously increased by my perusal of these family papers. She was a splendid specimen of an Englishwoman. Her courage, perseverance, energy, and unselfishness are amazing, and a really bright example to all who can appreciate them. By the way I do not think that one would find in many families, a son who preserved the bulk of his mother's letters covering a period of nearly forty years! There are letters from Mrs Trollope to her eldest son at Winchester written in 1824, seventy years ago. . . .

This letter brings us back, full circle, to the mother of Tom and Anthony, and with it I will close the series. As the reader will have seen, much of the correspondence deals with trivia; but the view it gives of Victorian author-publisher relations over a long period of years is very characteristic both of the Trollopes and their times. The vigor that informed these letters still lingers, enlivening what are otherwise merely long-forgotten business transactions.

Trollope as Dramatist

In 1850 an unsuccessful novelist sat down and wrote a play. He worked over it as conscientiously as he could, and hopefully sent the result, which he called *The Noble Jilt*, to a manager. But let him tell the story himself:

"I believe that I did give the best of my intellect to the play, and I must own that when it was completed it pleased me much. I copied it, and re-copied it, touching it here and touching it there, and then sent it to my very old friend, George Bartley the actor, who had when I was in London been stage-manager of one of the great theatres, and who would I thought, for my own sake and for my mother's, give me the full benefit of his professional experience.

"I have now before me the letter which he wrote to me,—a letter which I have read a score of times. It was altogether condemnatory. . . . a blow in the face! But I accepted the judgment loyally, and said not a word on the subject to any one."

However painful the criticism, the work was not destroyed. In 1863, when Anthony Trollope had become one of the most popular authors in England, he thriftily exhumed his *Noble Jilt*, and from its dry bones constructed the excellent novel *Can You Forgive Her?* It is important to observe that he added a new element: ". . . that which endears the book to me is the first presentation which I made in it of Plantagenet Palliser, with his wife, Lady Glencora"—and to these figures the book owes much of its attractiveness. The greater scope

Anthony Trollope had a few copies of Did He Steal It? *privately printed in 1869, but did not publish it. In 1952, when the Friends of the Princeton University Library decided to produce an edition of it, this article appeared therein as an introduction.*

permitted by the length of a sprawling novel was always to improve his work.

In 1869, nearly twenty years after that first attempt, Trollope made another effort at writing a comedy, and this time he reversed the former process. He chose the main plot from the rich and crowded canvas of *The Last Chronicle of Barset*, which in his *Autobiography* he calls "the best novel I have written," and goes on to say:

> "Some year or two after the completion of *The Last Chronicle*, I was asked by the manager of a theatre to prepare a piece for his stage, and I did so, taking the plot of this novel. I called the comedy *Did He Steal It?* But my friend the manager did not approve of my attempt. My mind at this time was less attentive to such a matter than when dear old George Bartley nearly crushed me by his criticism,—so that I forget the reason given."

The indifference is probably exaggerated. Trollope tends to keep intensity of personal feeling out of his life story— an assertion which may be tested by reference to the year 1872, when for the third and last time he was involved with a play. His own account is this:

> "During my absence in Australia, he [Charles Reade] took the plot of a novel of mine, and, adapting it very cleverly to the stage, brought it out, with a notice on the title, that it was by 'Anthony Trollope and Charles Reade.' This he did without any concert with me, and without any former partnership . . . I may say without any word having ever passed between us in reference to joint workmanship. I felt myself bound to repudiate the play by writing to the newspapers. . . . this unauthorized use of my name on a playbill angered me. I could not, however, make him understand that he had done wrong, and could only escape from the absurdity of a personal quarrel with a man I esteemed by suggesting to him that nothing more should be said about it by either of us."

But this mild statement does not begin to describe the raging tempest that took place, with both authors writing to the newspapers and to third parties rather than to each other. Reviews charging the play with indecency did not help matters, and the litigious Reade sued one critic for libel. The two did quarrel, in spite of what Trollope says, and reconciliation was not effected until 1877; in the intervening years they were once or twice seen at the Garrick playing whist in frigid silence. Most of the trouble arose, of course, because Reade did not try to obtain Trollope's acquiescence in the beginning; instead, he waited until less than a month before the performance and then cooly wrote:

> "I would not have taken this liberty without consulting you if you had been accessible. Having done it I now propose to give the inventor that just honor, which has too often been denied him in theatrical announcements. This will, I venture to think, do you no discredit, and will open the theatre to you, should you at any time feel disposed to enter it relying on your own talent only."

Reade's action was then legally permissible, but such a letter would have infuriated Trollope in any case; and with two unproduced plays in his desk he must have been especially lacerated by the patronizing last sentence. *Could* Reade have known . . . ? At all events, Trollope refused to have any connection with the stage performance, and whatever interest he may once have had in being a dramatist spluttered out in a welter of bad temper and broken friendship.

But there was no real literary loss. His talent did not lie in the theater, and any consideration of *Did He Steal It?* will be almost certain to end in wonder that so gifted a writer could so mistake his métier. His peculiar virtue as a novelist is his ability to present a panoramic view of mid-nineteenth-century English life, and his method was first to think out his characters clearly in advance, and then to write at top speed, letting the plot take care of itself. Too frequently this resulted in a rather shapeless structure, but neither he nor his readers cared about that. What he felt he owed them was a story solidly compact of episode and the interplay of character; and his readers were, and still are, content with the slow unfolding of his elaborate narratives. When all his faults have been listed, he remains one of the best storytellers in the language.

But in the conciseness necessary for a good play he had no skill whatever. His leisurely way with fiction has been compared to that of a shop assistant cutting off lengths of material; and he was totally unable to reveal the essential qualities of human nature through continuous dramatic action, or even to sharpen his dialogue so that its pace might be quickened without being forced. One of his late novels begins with a lament about the difficulties of exposition:

"I would that it were possible so to tell a story that a reader should beforehand know every detail of it up to a certain point, or be so circumstanced that he might be supposed to know. In telling the little novelettes of our life, we commence our narrations with the presumption that these details are borne in mind. . . . But such stories as those I have to tell cannot be written after that fashion. We novelists are constantly twitted with being long; and to the gentlemen who condescend to review us, and who take up our volumes with a view to business rather than pleasure, we must be infinite in length and tedium. But the story must be made intelligible from the beginning, or the real novel readers will not like it. The plan of jumping at once into the middle has been often tried, and sometimes seductively enough for a chapter or two; but the writer still has to hark back, and to begin again from the beginning—not always very comfortably after the abnormal brightness of his few opening pages; and the reader, who is then involved in some ancient family history, or long local explanation, feels himself to have been defrauded."

These, surely, are the words of one who would always find the dramatic form intolerably cramping, and who required for his best work the spaciousness of a long novel, in which character and situation could be built up with innumerable subtle strokes.

The Last Chronicle of Barset was Trollope's own favorite among his novels; it is as long as any he ever wrote, and the list of dramatis personae is greater, the complexity of happenings is more involved, than in his other works. It deals not merely with an obscure clergyman's sufferings when accused of theft, but with the impact of that accusation on the parish, the cathedral town, the county, and even London and beyond. The chapters spread out like ripples on a pond, until opinions have been canvassed in the bishop's palace and the laborer's cottage, and a whole society has been made to describe itself. But since a dramatic version must perforce be restricted to the supposed theft, drastic surgery was needed to fit the story to the Procrustean bed of the stage. "The pruning-knife? zounds!—the axe!" as Mr. Puff observes of his mangled tragedy; and in truth, of the noble oak which was *The Last Chronicle* little is left but a stump.

For this farewell to the county he had created Trollope brought back all the surviving characters of the earlier tales of Barsetshire, and for good measure threw in a new group of Londoners. Not only have these newcomers been excised from *Did He Steal It?*, but of all the old friends only the Crawleys and their daughter Grace remain. Though figures resembling the bishop and Mrs. Proudie are there, more than their name has been changed, and indeed a profound difference has occurred in Mr. Crawley himself. Apparently Trollope felt that the stage was not a suitable medium in which to exhibit the difficulties of a clergyman charged with stealing, and he carefully removed the Church of England atmosphere which had colored the novel and given it unity.

Mr. Crawley is now a schoolmaster, and the Proudies are represented by Mr. and Mrs. Goshawk, the local magistrate and his termagant wife. Something of the old situation is left, but how flat it seems! Young love will be served, and so Grace has her suitor, but instead of Major Grantly, she is provided with Captain Oakley, a son of Mrs. Goshawk by a former marriage. Thus the Goshawks substitute for the Grantlys as well as the Proudies, but the telescoping is too violent, and the Goshawks do not share the vitality of their prototypes.

It is true that a few of the novel's big scenes remain: for instance, Mr. Crawley's magnificent "Peace, woman!" which puts Mrs. Proudie to rout for the only time in her history. But alas! in *Did He Steal It?* Mr. Crawley unfortunately uses the same words to his wife before addressing them to Mrs. Goshawk, so that their effect is altogether ruined. On the other hand, the interview in which Mr. Crawley seeks for sympathy from the brickmaker is still vivid, and contains the familiar line "It's dogged as does it," which Trollope liked well enough to repeat at the final curtain.

A new name occurs in the play which will repay some inspection because of the light it throws on Trollope's mind at work. Mrs. Crawley's cousin, who volunteers to help his relatives, is at first downcast by Mr. Crawley's inability to recall how he obtained the ill-omened £20, but brightens at the thought of retaining the barrister Jacky Joram. Now there is no mention of this name in *The Last Chronicle*, but the scene is developed at some length for the sake of its comic effect. The audience is made clearly to understand that Joram cares only about winning a verdict and nothing at all about abstract justice, which, of course, grates on the scrupulously honest Mr. Crawley. "You mustn't tell Joram the truth, you know. It's the worst thing in the world! When a counsel once knows the truth he ain't half himself." Joram is never brought on the stage; but the slight sketch remained in Trollope's memory, and in *Ralph the Heir* (1871) Jacky Joram is a barrister at the hearing of the election petition. *John Caldigate* (1879) reveals him as Sir John Joram, defending the hero on a bigamy charge and telling his client that "no statement from your lips ought to affect me in the least. . . . It is not for me to believe or disbelieve anything in this matter. . . . It will be my duty not to make the jury believe you, who, in your position, will not be expected even to tell the truth; but to induce them, if possible, to disbelieve the witnesses against you who will be on their oath." That grain of mustard seed tossed on the stony ground of *Did He Steal It?* has grown—not very high, certainly, but with a beautiful consistency that displays Trollope's habit of living with and cherishing even the minor people of whom he wrote.

But of necessity there is very little in the play that is new. For the most part it is a scissors-and-paste job: nearly all the dialogue is transcribed directly from the novel, and the joints are plainly seen wherever cuts were found desirable. A trifling example will suffice: Grace tells her mother that she has rejected her lover, saying, "Shall I do him harm, because he would do me good?" And Mrs. Crawley answers, "The service he requires is your love in return for his." It is an oddly phrased reply; and a glance at the source reveals what has happened. There Grace asks, "Shall I injure him because he wants to do me a service?" and her mother says, "If he loves you, Grace, the service he will require will be your love in return." An attempt at shortening the speeches has resulted merely in a *non sequitur*, and emphasizes the haste and carelessness with which Trollope composed the play.

Though *Did He Steal It?* seems so inept that nothing good can be said of it, yet, after all, it is the work of a distinguished author; why then did he fail so utterly in this second effort at comedy?

One answer is that he did not. Trollope does not state why the manager rejected the piece, but it may be reasonably assumed that he had profitably produced worse plays. For nearly a century the English drama lapsed into undistinguished routine. No play of significance had been produced since Sheridan ceased to write for the theater. Knowles and Bulwer Lytton provided Macready with successes, but they were for the most part personal triumphs of the actor. (He even made a success out of Byron's *Werner*.) And the performances of Robertson's *Society*, *Ours*, and *Caste* in 1865, 1866, and 1867 are important historically more for their stagecraft than for any creative ability on the part of the author. There would still be a weary period of punning farces and sentimental melodrama before new ideas were to bring about a fresh concept of playwriting.

Trollope was no innovator, no reformer, but a man of his time, and it is in no way surprising that he should turn out a comedy representative of its period, with stock characters and a perfunctory denouement. He was not the sort to break new ground; and theatrical producers are not as a rule eager for radical changes. The novelties they like are tried and true. But it is clear that the manager did want a play with some of the qualities that had caused the publishers to pay Trollope £3000 for *The Last Chronicle*. Is it not also probable that the manager would feel that an audience, seeing the eminent name on a playbill, would expect those qualities and would resent their absence? *Did He Steal It?* is not unlike many plays of its time; but it is very unlike a Trollope novel, and surely that is what the manager hoped for.

And yet, much as everyone would prefer it to resemble the novels, this stillborn play has an interest of its own. Its prolific author was no dramatist, neither did he seem to understand his own genius. Only through trial and many errors did he find the sort of fiction which he could do superlatively well; and having found it, he deserted it regularly. To him writing was writing, it mattered not what, and in the intervals between novels he turned out articles, short stories, lectures, travel books, newsletters, biographies—and two plays, one of them while still a fumbling beginner, and the other, now at hand, while at the peak of his career. But all these deviations from his true course are nevertheless part of his work, and for those who wish to know thoroughly the man and his achievement, this souvenir of his mistaken judgment is no less instructive and no less typical than the great novel from which it was made.